FROM OBSCURITY TO OBLIVION

From Obscurity to Oblivion:
Neglected Books and
their Forgotten Authors

GREGORY STEPHENSON

Ober-Limbo Verlag

Grateful acknowledgement is made to the editors of *Foundation* and *Velocities,* in which certain of the essays in this volume have previously appeared.

Published by Ober-Limbo Verlag
Heidelberg, Germany

ISBN 978-87-971569-7-1

Cover photo, design & layout by
Birgit Stephenson

For Birgit

génie méconnue

"Reality, life, experience, concreteness, immediacy, use what word you will, exceeds our logic, overflows and surrounds it."

William James
A Pluralistic Universe

CONTENTS

INTRODUCTION

As to why certain worthy books end as unread and unremembered, while other books – often far less worthy – achieve brief glory or perennial popularity or at least manage to remain in print, perhaps the most obvious explanation is the operation of chance. Given the enormous volume of books printed every year, year upon year, it would seem inevitable that a certain portion – including a portion of the best of them – should at some stage after their publication get lost in the rush, the shuffle and the crush, and thereafter be forgotten. A slighting review or no review at all, unfortunate timing, an obscure or unappealing title, an unattractive binding or dust wrapper, poor promotion or poor distribution on the part of the publisher – the causes of their neglect may be any one of many but the fate shared by such unlucky books is the same: oblivion.

Or it may be that the fate of certain worthy books is not altogether a matter of chance, that it is instead a question of the complacency of critics and of the reading public. Indeed, with regard to particular undeservedly neglected books – those of an unsettling potential, those that might subvert reader repose – I sometimes wonder whether their neglect may not be the result of a species of unconscious resistance to or evasion of them on the part of reviewers and readers. But how shall we determine the hidden mechanisms of defense that underlie reader *non-response*? I note, however, that a common trait among the books treated in the following pages is their unsettling quality, their power to provoke in the mind of the reader disturbing doubts concerning primary human issues: the nature of identity, reality, morality, authority, the question of human destiny. And I note, too, that the disquieting effect of the books presented in the following derives from their shared engagement in extreme situations and states of mind, their excursions into the borderlands of human experience.

In a study titled *The Palm at the End of the Mind* (2009) the author (not the deceased entertainer of opprobrious reputation) Michael Jackson has written of what he names "limit experiences," that is to say "those situations in life where we come up against the limits of our language, our strength, and our knowledge," those circumstances in which our "habits are ruptured" and our minds are "thrown open to new ways of understanding our being-in-the world." He further notes that such border situations – painful and distressing as they are – may have as their motive power an unconscious impulse to destroy the constraints of the quotidian world, an impulse to liberate ourselves from the habits and routines that confine us, and thus to impel us toward moments of realization, of recognition, of revelation. (Might not, then, the avoidance of such limit situations, even unto the vicarious experience of them, also derive from an unconscious impulse?)

Predicaments, plights, ordeals, shattering events and encounters, madness, terror, imprisonment, violence, obsession, despair – the narrators and protagonists of the half dozen overlooked, underrated books I have chosen to promote here have all for a season been confined in one or another region of the netherworld, the inward infernos of the mind. Yet in each instance the dark underworld proves to be a place of existential self-encounter, the sojourn there an occasion of redemption and transformation. The scorched travellers return from their perilous night journey having recognized the falsity of the self they lived before the advent of their descent, and having turned away from that false and empty self, that illusion of selfhood. They return having discovered in themselves the germ of another and deeper identity.

The authors of these books offer in their works no facile answers, no glib formulae for achieving felicity or sanctity. Rather, they profess only to have known the ways of ignorance and error, and to have awakened at last to another order of values, and to the possibilities of life and growth inherent in that order. It is to be hoped that the books presented here can serve to recall to our minds that which we are inclined to forget or suppress while occupied in the sphere of ordinary, practical existence, reminding us of higher principles and deeper truths, wider perspectives and larger potentials, and offering us a clarified sense of what is authentic and essential in life.

"A work of power and brilliance…"
—LOS ANGELES TIMES
OPERATORS and THINGS
Barbara O'Brien
THE REAL-LIFE ADVENTURE THAT IS STRANGER THAN SCIENCE FICTION

The Wax Boom
GEORGE MANDEL

A PRISON
A PARADISE
BY LORAN HURNSCOT
—from KATHLEEN RAINE'S foreword

THE HOLE IN THE ZERO M.K. Joseph

PICADOR
Anna Kavan
ICE

FOUR SQUARE
5/-
Post Bellum Blues:
Finn MacMahon
A life of debauchery and corruption

WAYLAID FROM WITHIN:
Operators and Things

"Much Madness is divinest Sense –
To a discerning Eye –
Much Sense – the Starkest Madness –"
Emily Dickinson

Without forewarning or transition – like Alice suddenly tumbling down the rabbit hole or passing abruptly through the looking glass from one realm of existence to another – the narrator of this compelling autobiographical account awakens one morning to find herself in another world. Opening her eyes from sleep, in her own bedroom, Barbara O'Brien (a pseudonym for the author) sees three male figures standing at the foot of her bed. She learns from the intruders that they are "Operators," and that she – whom they regard as and refer to a "Thing" – has been selected by another more powerful Operator to be the subject of an experiment. "Things," she is told, are the many millions of human beings who inhabit the physical world, while "Operators" are entities who exist in a parallel world and who prey upon, play upon and secretly control Things. Conceived by a rogue Operator named Hadley, the experiment of which O'Brien is to be the unwilling and unlucky subject is designed to discover how a Thing will respond when "it" is made aware of the presence in the world of Operators and of their parasitic power over human minds. To this end, the three Operators in O'Brien's bedroom have come to deliver their message, projecting their appearance into her bedroom while their actual physical structures remain elsewhere.

Barbara is told that Burt, the elderly, conservative, dependable-looking man who first addresses her has, in fact, been her Operator in recent years, but that previous to that a sullen, dishevelled young man named Hinton – also present in the room – was her Operator. It is with him she must now become better acquainted, she is informed. ("It is necessary for the good of all concerned that you get to know Hinton better.") She must on no account reveal to other Things the existence of Operators. She also soon discovers that the Operators can read her thoughts. Nothing can be hidden from them. She has no secrets, neither past nor present, with which the Operators are unacquainted. Before many minutes have passed, however, the room in which they are speaking is attacked mentally by the "city council," the local legal authority of Operators. Hadley's experiment has been detected by the council and they have deemed it to be illegal and hazardous to the whole historical relationship between Operators and Things. Fearing that Barbara will ultimately reveal her newly acquired knowledge of the existence and activities of Operators, the council mean to kill her, doing so by manipulating her mind in such a way as to coerce her to commit suicide. Barbara is urged by her Operators to flee the council's jurisdiction, though even should she succeed in evading them, she is told, her chances of survival are only about one in three hundred. She immediately packs a bag, flees to the bus station and buys a ticket to the nearest large city.

Thus begins the author's anxious, erratic, six-month-long flight across and even outside of the United States. Having withdrawn her savings, O'Brien travels by bus and train down to New Orleans, thence to Texas, then to a cabin in a remote rural area of an unnamed northern state. She next takes a plane to a city in northern Canada, but soon returns by bus to Washington State. Journeying from there to Butte, Montana, she quickly removes to Salt Lake City, then seeks refuge in a city in California, from which she subsequently flees but to which she later returns. In the course of her travels, she is institutionalized once but soon (with the help of her Operators) talks her way out of the psychiatric ward to which she is confined. The voices and visual projections of various Operators are ever present to her. Her knowledge of their laws and customs and their capabilities slowly increases, and in the course of her journey she encounters several score of them; some are members of organizations, others are free-lancers, most are malevolent or callous at best, but a few are pleasant and benign, offering her reassurances and sound advice. She learns to conceive of her situation and her mental condition in terms employed by the Operators: "shack," "board," "shield," "latticework," "scalloping," "battlement," "charter," "flies," "bill of resuscitation," and other designations. All such terms are defined by the author as they occur in the text, and a glossary is provided as an appendix to the book.

After undergoing various forms of persecution inflicted upon her by scores of Operators and after enduring lengthy and complex legal proceedings in their courts, Barbara spontaneously recovers from her affliction. She is suddenly and entirely free of her relentless visual and auditory hallucinations and the convictions of verisimilitude that accompany them. But, she is, by no means, fully recovered. Her mind is impaired, her former identity in abeyance. The author describes her consciousness during this immediate post-delusion period as "the dry beach." Torpid and lethargic, she is devoid of initiative, thought, memory and emotion, scarcely capable of functioning in a world which now seems indecipherable to her. She can neither make sense of the written texts she attempts to read, nor of films she tries to see, nor of the speech of voices on the radio. Even traffic signals and simple newspaper headlines perplex her.

Like "waves" (as she likens them) upon the "dry beach" of her mind, by slow increments recognition and understanding of the world return to her. During this period, she is also guided in her daily life by a mental phenomenon she names "Something." When Barbara is confronted with a problem, great or small, a wise and benign "Something" from somewhere below the level of her diminished consciousness urges her to undertake specific actions which invariably result in solutions to the problems. In this manner, she locates misplaced objects, retrieves forgotten items, buys necessary supplies in shops, practices economies, and finds employment. The urges she receives from "Something" are much more on the order of commands than hints or nudges. At times the directives from "Something" take the form of visual images. "Something," she writes, "obviously was determined to have its own way." At length, though, reason and emotion return to her and she is again intact, cured, sane. But – as I shall indicate – she is not unchanged by her strange journey.

Having fully recovered, O'Brien is keen to learn something concerning the nature and cause of the harrowing experience through which she has lived. She visits the local city library to obtain textbooks on psychology and studies of schizophrenia. Ultimately, to her disappointment, she finds the books to be of little utility to her, as there would seem to prevail among authorities in the fields of psychology and psychiatry considerable disagreement as to either the origins of or effective treatments for the disorder with which she was lately afflicted.

The absence of satisfactory scholarly explanations for her delusional episode prompts O'Brien to seek within herself an understanding of her malady. She begins by typing out a detailed account of her prolonged misadventure. In doing so, she notes significant parallels between certain of her experiences, perceptions and emotions in her place of work (previous to the advent of her phantom persecutors) and those she has known in the world of the Operators. Up to the morning of the intrusion into her life of the Operators, O'Brien had worked for seven years in the design department of a large enterprise – the Knox Corporation – somewhere in the Midwestern United States. During this time, she witnesses a number of incidents in which ruthlessly ambitious employees, whom she privately thinks of as "hook-operators," are successful in being promoted to lucrative managerial positions through having employed deceit, innuendo and other devious and underhanded tactics to sabotage the careers of their competitors or superiors. She notes how "clever, ingenious and resourceful" such hook-operators are, how they are able to objectify other humans and conceive of others solely as obstacles to be removed, how they seem to have an instinct or "nose" for the vulnerabilities of others, "soft spots" that can then be cunningly exploited for their own advantage.

The imagery O'Brien deploys in relating her accounts of the hook-operators she has observed discloses a profound sense of unease and dismay with such behaviour. She dwells on the cruel operation of the invisible hook on which victims are caught and on their hopeless thrashings and agonies once hooked. She views the machinations of the hook-operators in terms of weaponry and physical attacks: backbones are cracked, hooks once inserted are then twisted in the victims; metaphorically, throats are cut, heads cleft, needles are inserted, knives, hatchets and even a broadaxe are employed, victims bleed. The hook-operators themselves are depicted as subhuman or diabolical in the cruel execution of their malicious skills, one of them is represented as having a cloven foot, another has a "cold, spiderish" stare.

O'Brien is aware, too, of the motivation behind the sly, slow, deliberate viciousness of the hook-operators. They are pursuing money, power and prestige. Ironically, there is a sense in which they themselves are hooked by their aims and ambitions. The author also recognizes that although she abhors the means employed by hook-operators, she shares with them certain similar objectives. Previous to the appearance of the Operators, she was, she writes, "making an excellent salary and had a clear opportunity to receive an even more excellent salary within a short time." She then adds: "These are the things with which you hook yourself." At the same time, as a psychic response to her appalled observations of the hook-operators, she developed a terror of coming to work every morning, a terror she attempted to deny and suppress.

O'Brien wonders why in the course of our socialization or our education we are never briefed on the presence among us of hook-operators, but concedes that given the competitive nature of the corporate world and of society and the world in general, hook-operators are perfectly adapted to their environment. Following her long nightmare journey in the company of the Operators, O'Brien can view her previous career in perspective. She can see that in the manner of a dream her delusional episode was symbolic in form, a clarification in dramatic, metaphoric terms of the human situation, the conditions of life, where some prey while others are preyed upon. Indeed, there is at one point in the narrative an exchange between Barbara and an Operator in which the Operator observes that: "a

Thing can be influenced chiefly because of its desire for money and power. An Operator's security and self-esteem revolve about Operator's points just as a Thing's revolves about money." The Operator then further comments that "Operators and Things are motivated by similar desires. We're both in the soup, Operators and Things alike."

From her inward eclipse, two vital insights are derived by O'Brien. She comes to understand that in her former career as an employee in the design department of the Knox Corporation, her own covertly nourished cupidity and ambition constituted a hook that she inserted into herself, into her spirit. She was, in this manner and to this degree, herself responsible for summoning the Operators. "I walked out of Knox," she writes, "with a hook in my back that was entirely of my own making. When I finally pulled it out and had a good look at it, I decided that nobody could have stuck it in my back except myself, and the only satisfaction I got was that I was able to pull it out myself, and see clearly the shape of it." This brave and honest self-assessment seems to me a precious prize to have been retrieved by the author from out of her psychic shipwreck.

A second valuable truth grasped and adopted by O'Brien comes to her during the period after her full recovery when she takes a job working in the field of publicity. She soon perceives that – as in her former place of employment – the office where she now works is abundantly furnished with an array of back-stabbing, hatchet-wielding, hook-operators. She reflects that on the strength of her extensive and attentive observations of hook-operators in two enterprises and in two dimensions, she might now for her own advancement and satisfaction execute similar maneuvers herself. Indeed, studying those around her in the office, the author can see several inviting targets-of-opportunity. She resists, however, the pull of this temptation, declining to join the ranks of the predators, "the realists," suspecting that their cynical attitudes and heartless wiles and devices must ultimately cost them the forfeiture of their human souls: "I looked objectively at the knife and dispassionately considered, nothing at all of the sharpness of the edge, but what would happen to the shape of the hand that held the knife. The evidence of what I might become in time was clear. I had only to look around the office in any direction to see it."

A deeper reading by the author of her journey through inner darkness discloses to her motives for her madness more profound than merely her revulsion at the Hobbesian nature of life in the world. Examining and carefully analyzing her detailed memories of the radically unsettling experience she has had, she is intrigued by her recollection of how at the very outset of her sojourn in the realm of the Operators, she was told by the staid, sedate Burt that "It is necessary for the good of all concerned that you get to know Hinton better." O'Brien was particularly unsettled to hear this because, it will be remembered, while elderly Burt seemed to her a judicious, respectable, reliable man, Hinton struck her as "a real weirdo," unkempt in appearance and sullen and truculent in manner. His every surly glance, his very presence caused her to feel uneasy. Burt, she was informed, had been her Operator in recent years, but in a time before that, her Operator had been Hinton. "You know him well," Burt insists, "you used to know him better."

Having read widely and deeply on the topic of schizophrenia, and being inclined to be sceptical regarding the various one-dimensional explanations of its causes and nature (a form of biochemical self-poisoning, a dysfunction of the adrenal gland, the thyroid gland, an endocrine imbalance, sex repression) the author attempts to understand her strange experience in more practical, personal terms. O'Brien senses that her turbulent psychotic episode was purposive. It had teleological significance. In an earnest, analytical spirit, she asks of herself a vital question: "What was the mistake I had made somewhere in the past? What monster had I kept under weights in the unconscious? Significantly, it had been a monster that had lain low until it chose to strike ... until it was large enough to crack the cage and walk giant-size into my mind."

With close attention, the author begins to interpret the events and contents of her disorder, to construe and elucidate its elements as if it were a drama or a literary text. The figure of Hinton, she believes, is a key to the meaning of the story. Hinton alone was present from first to last, and Hinton alone among the Operators had occasioned her the greatest unease. Why should she have been informed that "for the good of all concerned" she must improve her acquaintance with him? And what did it mean that before Burt, Hinton had been her Operator? First, O'Brien concludes that Operators represent components of the unconscious mind, while Things are the conscious mind. She concludes that sober, sedate Burt with his distinguished appearance, her most recent Operator, embodied the restrained, social-conformist attitudes that she had permitted to govern her behaviour for years. She had (perhaps already in adolescence) forsaken the unkempt, undaunted, non-conformist spirit of her childhood, as embodied in the figure of Hinton, by whose inspirations and motivations she was once guided, for the quiet, steady Burt, thus taking on for utilitarian purposes the identity of a more socially acceptable persona. Hinton, "the cat who walked alone, who did things his own way," was the rejected, discarded self without whom she was incomplete and must remain inauthentic and unfulfilled; he was the vital missing component of her personality.

A complementary parallel to the necessary re-integration of Hinton is suggested in her complex and prolonged psychodrama by the recurrence of the terms "horse" and "bronco," which are applied to her (but never explained) by certain of the Operators she encounters or whom she overhears discussing her. She learns from them on more than one occasion that she is a natural "bronco" who has become a "horse." A bronco, of course, is unbroken, untamed, bucking predators off its back, acting without inhibition, according to its nature and instincts. A horse, then, in a metaphoric sense, is an animal whose spirit has been broken so as to be tractable and useful; it has been domesticated, made docile, brought under control; it allows itself to be ridden upon. Over the course of her distressful adventure ("full of fear and shock" to borrow a phrase from Robert Graves) Barbara O'Brien summons forth defiance and resistance to her plight, repossessing in the process her original propensity to be a "bronco," a quality of spirit she suppressed under the Operatorship of prudent, judicious Burt.

Strange to say, ultimately, O'Brien's psychological crisis is transformative, redemptive. Her psychic disintegration gives rise in the end to a reintegration of dissociated fragments of her unconscious identity and, having given expression to repressed forces within herself, she emerges from her breakdown possessing greater strength, stability and harmony of spirit. Her mind has found a new equilibrium. She has become reoriented, centered. She has, moreover, achieved a deeper, broader view of human consciousness and its potentials.

Significant parallels may be seen between O'Brien's experience and certain patterns of myth. The archetype of the Night-Sea Crossing provides one such analogy: the passage of the sun through a lower abyss of darkness and its subsequent resurrection. (See *A Dictionary of Symbols* by J.E. Cirlot, Philosophical Library, New York, 1962.) Another correspondence may be seen with the motif of the *katabasis* or descent into a netherworld inhabited by supernatural beings, a downward journey in quest of knowledge or benefit, as undertaken by Gilgamesh, Orpheus, Aeneas, Odysseus and Dante, among others. Joseph Campbell, author of the seminal study of myth, *The Hero with a Thousand*

Faces (1949) has observed that "the imagery of the schizophrenic fantasy perfectly matches that of the mythological hero journey." (See "Schizophrenia – the Inward Journey" in *Myths to Live By* by Joseph Campbell, Paladin Books, London, 1985.) The hero journey, it will be remembered, consists of three phases: (1) separation (2) initiation, and (3) return. A hero sets forth from the familiar world of commonplace reality and enters into a realm of supernatural entities and forces, ordeals are undergone and overcome, and victory is won. The hero then returns from these adventures bearing "boons" for the community from which he departed. In common with the hero journey, the schizophrenic breakdown, in Campbell's view, may be seen as "an inward and backward journey to recover something missed or lost, and to restore, thereby, a vital balance." ("Schizophrenia – the Inward Journey." This seems an apt description of the author's perilous passage through her salutary malady.

Barbara O'Brien returns from her descent into the underworld, her hero journey, with new strength and knowledge. *Operators and Things,* the record of her fraught, metanoiac journey, is her boon to the community. And, although disruptive and acutely distressing, her experience has also been of benefit to her. It has caused her to shed her false, socially-conformist, compliant self and to recover her original "bronco" spirit. She has become aware of and overcome a number of debilitating psychological habits, and has examined and mastered her own desires for money, prestige and power. And she has discovered within herself unsuspected potentialities and abilities: at one point during her recovery, as if by dictation, she swiftly and spontaneously writes a novel of sixty thousand words. For a period during her recovery, she also experiences instances of precognition, knowing beforehand whom she will encounter and what they will say to her. The most striking example of precognition occurs when "Something" dispatches her to Las Vegas with only five dollars in her pocket. Guided by "Something" into a particular casino and to a roulette table there, she is informed by the same inner power to place bets on particular numbers. She wins six times in a row. Then, the urges to place bets and the foreknowledge cease. But by this time, she has won sufficient money to continue to support herself for weeks to come.

Barbara O'Brien's vivid, lucid account of her madness and its spontaneous remission brings into view new perspectives on the nature of consciousness and the self. Her book provokes questions with profound implications, questions not easily susceptible of definitive answers. What is the nature of perception? What portion of what we take to be reality has objective existence and what portion is subjective projection? Who is the hidden Director of O'Brien's psychodrama? Who within her is it that conceived and co-ordinated the unfolding script of her complex delusions, bringing together "ninety-nine assistants," each with a name, a face and a function, with the aim of deceiving and instructing her? Who deep within O'Brien's mind is the Witness, the Invigilator? How deep is the *within* within us? What are its boundaries?

Operators and Things, singular as it is, appeared in 1958, in the context of postwar American culture, an aspect of which was an interest in frontiers of the mind. Other books concerning anomalies and potentials of the human mind appeared in the same era. Aldous Huxley's pioneering work on visionary consciousness, *The Doors of Perception* was published in 1954, followed in 1956 by a companion volume, *Heaven and Hell.* Morey Bernstein's fascinating narrative of a case of hypnotic regression, *The Search for Bridey Murphy,* was published in 1956, and later released as a feature motion picture. An account of the phenomenon of multiple personality disorder titled *The Three Faces of Eve* by Corbett H. Thigpen and Hervey M. Cleckley appeared in 1957, and was also turned into a feature film. In January of 1961, a book titled *Exploring Inner Space: Personal Experience Under LSD-25* by Jane Dunlap (nom-de-plume of Adelle Davis) was published, an early account of psychedelic therapy. Such reports from the mind's interior may be likened to the maps and ship's logs of bold navigators during the Age of Exploration.

Another topic of interest during the postwar period was the issue of conformity, which is clearly a central concern in *Operators and Things.* Popular books on this cultural anxiety published roughly contemporaneously with *Operators and Things* include: *The Lonely Crowd* (1950) by David Riesman and Nathan Glazer; *The Organization Man* (1956) by William F. Whyte; and *Must You Conform?* (1956) by Robert Lindner. Madness, too, was a prominent literary theme in the postwar era. It is a central motif in Allen

Ginsberg's celebrated poem *Howl* (1956) and in the poet Sylvia Plath's semi-autobiographical novel, *The Bell Jar* (1963) which is set in the 1950s and which was originally published under the pseudonym, Victoria Lucas. Out of their own raw, ruinous experience, postwar poets Robert Lowell ("My mind's not right") John Berryman, Ann Sexton ("Poetry led me by the hand out of madness") Delmore Schwartz and Theodore Roethke ("What's madness but nobility of soul / at odds with circumstance?") also treated the theme. Madness is also a principal theme in Ken Kesey's novel, *One Flew Over the Cuckoo's Nest* (1962.) Indeed, Kesey's novel has certain elements in common with O'Brien's account, including imagery of fog and machinery, fiends in human form, the themes of conformity and control, and the use of the term "combine." (These parallels may, of course, be coincidental or derive from similar experiences of the two authors. It may be, however, that Kesey was familiar with O'Brien's book and employed in his novel imaginatively altered facets of her narrative.)

Without pressing the case, it's worth mentioning, I think, and fair to say, that *Operators and Things* anticipates in significant ways the anti-psychiatry movement which was to come to the fore in the 1960s. In this regard, there is a statement regarding schizophrenia in R. D. Laing's *The Politics of Experience* (1967) that seems particularly apt to the experience of Barbara O'Brien: *"this voyage is not what we need to be cured of, but is in itself a natural way of healing our own appalling state of alienation called normality."* (Emphasis in the original.)

There is also a sense in which *Operators and Things* may be regarded as a modern version of the classic American "captivity narrative," a once-popular genre of autobiography centered upon the ordeal of a Euro-American woman who is taken prisoner by merciless, barbarous Indian "savages." The earliest and perhaps best known of these books is Mary Rowlandson's *Sovereignty and Goodness of God: A True History of the Captivity and Restoration of Mrs. Mary Rowlandson, taken prisoner by Narragansett Indians* (1682.) Captivity narratives recount the trials and suffering, redemption and return of the captives. Often they provide ethnographic details concerning the customs and mores of the author's exotic and seemingly inhuman captors. Barbara O'Brien's autobiographical account can be seen to follow a similar pattern. Like the earlier portrayals by captives of the Indians, O'Brien's chronicle of her captivity by Operators includes the journey motif, ordeals endured, self-examination, observations of an ethnographic or anthropological nature concerning her captors, ultimate deliverance from captivity, and a relation of profound psychological changes occasioned by the experience.

Few books convey with such candour and authority the strangeness, the otherness, the alienness of that which is to each of us most intrinsic and most intimate – our own minds. *Operators and Things* illuminates to readers unknown planes and precincts, realms and recesses of consciousness. Presences fearful and benign. It is a remarkable book, a work of enduring value.

Operators and Things: The Inner Life of a Schizophrenic published by Arlingon Books, Cambridge, Massachusetts, 1958. Reprinted in paperback format by Ace Books, New York, 1960.

THE WAR WITHIN THE WAR:
The Wax Boom

The Wax Boom by George Mandel concerns a group of American soldiers, "A" troop of a Mechanized Cavalry Group, engaged in combat operations in the Rhineland in December of 1944. The unit has seen action in North Africa, in Normandy, across France, through Belgium and into Germany. As a result of their prolonged, unrelieved exposure to combat, the members of the unit are perilously close to nervous exhaustion and psychic collapse.

The cause of the unit's unconscionably protracted assignment to the front line is the overweening ambition of the Group commander, Colonel B. Drexel Powell, who – by posing as an eager and aggressive leader – hopes to attract the favourable notice of his superiors at Corps Headquarters and thereby to enjoy advancement in his military career.

Colonel Powell's self-serving bravado is mirrored down the chain of command, from Captain Churney, the Colonel's blustering, posturing, cowardly aide, to Captain Stollman, the commanding officer of "A" Troop. Captain Stollman makes a great show of feeling keen disappointment and painful frustration at not being able to participate directly in the combat missions that his unit undertakes, but in fact he has no desire whatever to leave the safety and comfort of his command post and to endure the rigors and mortal perils of the front line. Indeed, it is Captain Stollman's fervent hope that by proving to Colonel Powell his adroitness as a tactician he can secure for himself an assignment further removed from the front line, as far to the rear and as far from the war as possible.

The soldiers of the unit, who, in campaign after campaign, actually do the fighting are repeatedly placed at risk in missions that are undertaken far less to serve the purposes of the allied war effort than to further the ambitions and designs of Colonel Powell and Captain Stollman. The combat soldiers of the unit, including those of the Second Platoon of "A" Troop which constitutes the focus of the novel, have become increasingly aware of their situation with regard to their commanding officers, but are helpless to affect any alteration or amelioration of their plight. In consequence, the men have grown cynical and resentful, and in the course of their long months of combat they have also grown desperate and full of dread. As individual soldiers and as a fighting unit they are nearing a state of nervous breakdown.

One symptom of the soldiers' precarious mental state is the growing urgency of their need for light during the hours of darkness, and their consequent obsession with finding wax from which to make candles for that purpose.

It is at this critical point in the morale of the unit that two catalytic agents are by chance introduced in the form of two fresh replacements, First Lieutenant Simmons and Private Atman. Simmons is an obtuse martinet and an inveterate poseur whose stubbornly, arrogantly uninformed conduct on the front line endangers and outrages the men. Atman is a slyly derisive young jester with a singular aptitude for finding wax and making candles. Diametrically different in character, these two soldiers – each in his own manner – exercise a decisive influence upon the unsound minds and morale of the three platoons of "A" troop.

Lieutenant Simmons's presumptuous, pretentious, supercilious and swaggering manner, coupled with his acute lack of a practical grasp of the realities of combat, serve to alienate from him all respect and allegiance of the men serving under him, and to inspire his NCOs, Sergeants Proctor and Riglioni, to commit open acts of insubordination, and indeed, to make outright threats against his life. The overt refusal on the parts of Proctor and Riglioni to submit to the authority of Simmons's rank provokes Captain Stollman to attempt to enforce obedience to Simmons by punishing both of the two NCOs and the men of their sections with additional hazardous duty. This action only serves further to undermine the morale of "A" Troop.

Private Atman's uncanny knack for finding wax in the ruins of German houses and buildings, and his talent for making candles seem at the outset to be a timely benefit to the psychological well-being of the Second Platoon – to which Atman is assigned – and to "A" Troop as a unit. The light from Atman's candles provides the men with a measure of tranquillity during the dread-haunted hours of the night and a respite from the horror of the war by enabling them in the glow of the candlelight to fantasize of home and loved ones. But what seems at first to be a boon reveals itself ultimately to be a kind of trap as the men become hypnotized by the flames, losing themselves in their fantasies and neglecting the duties necessary to their survival on the front line.

As the unit moves forward, deeper into German territory, enemy resistance intensifies. Sergeant Proctor is maimed terribly in one engagement with the enemy, while other members of the unit are killed in action or collapse at last in combat-induced dementia. One soldier in a state of psychotic reaction massacres a group of unarmed German civilians, old men, women and children. These horrific events, combined with the revelation of the full extent of Captain Stollman's shameless hypocrisy (he has contrived to have himself awarded the Silver Star medal for gallantry in action) move Sergeant Riglioni finally to open defiance and rebellion: he resigns his rank, reducing himself in grade to the rank of private. Riglioni further expresses his resistance by declining any longer to lead troops into battle. He is willing to follow, he says, but only if Stollman will lead – that is physically lead – the men in battle.

In their utter exhaustion of mind and spirit, and their profound disenchantment, the surviving members of the Second Platoon join Riglioni in his rebellion and they in turn are soon joined by members of the other platoons that constitute "A" Troop. Together they take shelter in a cellar, alternately sleeping and gazing entranced into the light of the large candles that Atman has formed, finding in the candle flames refuge from danger and distress, and ignoring both the sound of incoming artillery outside and the increasingly urgent orders issued from the command post.

The passive rebellion of the men of "A" Troop, amounting to a sort of lethargic mutiny, could not have come at a more critical, more inopportune hour, for outside their cellar the German counter-offensive is raging. As the artillery bombardment lifts, the German army is attacking in strength, with infantry supported by armor. By the time Riglioni and his men are roused at last from their stupor by the din of battle, and stumble forth from the shelter of their cellar to man their armoured vehicles and bring their weapons to bear upon the attacking enemy, it is too late. Their position is quickly overrun and "A" Troop is completely destroyed, except for one badly wounded survivor.

In *The Wax Boom* there are two wars taking place; there are two fronts, two enemies. There is the savage war that is waged against the German army, and there is the subtle war that is fought between soldiers who wear the same uniform and who profess allegiance to the same cause. This latter contest is waged, inconspicuously and insidiously, furtively and surreptitiously, between those who are ruthless, hypocritical opportunists, and those whom they strive to dupe, to exploit, to manipulate and to sacrifice.

Vividly and powerfully, George Mandel renders the dread and wretchedness of life on the frontlines in the European Theatre of Operation. The author's sharp, intense descriptions of ground combat, the noise and havoc, the hallucinatory terror, the barely suppressed hysteria, convey a nightmare quality that is unforgettable. Equally haunting and moving is the author's evocation of the sickly horror and the clammy, eerie fear that permeate the mind of the combat soldier, who with a species of superstitious dread come to regard the enemy as an "enormous phantom," a spectral and obscene entity, whose individual component parts – the German soldiers – are yet repeatedly, inexplicably revealed to be no more than mere humans, miserable and vulnerable: "men of various ages, faces full of wives and mothers ... feeble, futile sons and fathers."

As a depiction of the appalling realities of combat, and of the agony and bitterness, the terror and despair, the humor and pity, that make up the life of the frontline G.I., *The Wax Boom* is a work of very considerable achievement. But, as I have suggested above, Mandel's novel is concerned with more than the war itself; it is concerned with the character of society and its institutions, and ultimately with the nature of the human spirit. These larger themes emerge from the motivations and actions of the novel's characters.

Two clusters of characters constitute the moral poles of the novel, two groups which may be called the Powell-Stollman alliance and the Riglioni affiliation. The former group consists of those in positions of authority (together with their allies and associates) who are able to insulate themselves from the terror and violence of the war, and who seek to employ such power as they possess in the furtherance of their personal goals, specifically promotion and advancement, that is to say in the pursuit of greater power. The latter group seeks only to win the war, to survive and to return home.

The foremost representative of the Powell-Stollman alliance is, of course, Colonel B. Drexel Powell whose avidness for reputation and for higher rank has caused his men to be kept in action on the frontline beyond any reasonable or permissible length of time. The casualties due to combat fatigue, the atrocities that are committed by the men under his command are the direct consequence of his ambition. The colonel's characteristic white raincoat suggests the "whited sepulchre" of the Bible, the very image of hypocrisy, white on the outside but all corruption within: "outwardly ye appear righteous unto men, but within ye are full of hypocrisy and iniquity" (Matthew 23:27) For all his bellicose bluster and marital swaggering, the Colonel takes every possible precaution to ensure his own safety, from the wide rubber band which he wears on his helmet to conceal his insignia of rank from the eyes of possible enemy snipers, to the smokepots among whose protective screen he hides his presence while his unit is in the assault. Moreover, Colonel Powell is only very seldom to be found in any proximity to the front line, and then only during brief periods of quiet. Clearly, the Colonel's pompous motto – "Courage is a matter of decision" – must either be seen as the ultimate expression of self-deception or as a smokescreen as concealing as any produced by the smokepots.

A worthy disciple of Colonel Powell is his subordinate, Captain Stollman. While not inclined to the exaggerated and rather obvious posturings of the

Colonel, Stollman is fully the equal of his commanding officer both in maintaining maximum possible distance to the actual dangers and bloodletting of the war and in terms of cynical manipulation of the lives of others with -the object of attaining his own private aims. Coaxing, cajoling, conning, bribing and threatening his sub-ordinates while carefully courting favour with his superiors, Stollman is a shrewd, shameless, self-serving hypocrite, and "a super-realist, of all possible enemies the deadliest."

A far less accomplished but no less confirmed dissembler is Captain Churney, aide to Colonel Powell. Churney affects the bluff and hearty air of a devil-may-care warrior, sports pearl-handled pistols, but is never to be found closer to the front line than the safe confines of the Group Command Post, located well beyond the maximum range of even the most powerful enemy artillery. Except under armed escort he is even afraid to visit the men of his own unit. A kind of caricature of Colonel Powell and Captain Stollman, Churney is both contemptible and pathetic in the conspicuousness of his sycophancy and his cowardice.

Yet so compelling and convincing is the specious rhetoric and martial posturing of Powell and Stollman in the eyes of certain less discerning, more obtuse troopers, that the Colonel and the Captain find among certain of the junior officers of the unit, eager, admiring dupes to do their bidding so that hey can remain in the safety of the rear. Two such obliging tools of Powell and Stollman are Lieutenants Morgdahl and Simmons.

Morgdahl and Simmons represent all those avid, gullible souls who without question, without reflection have accepted the set of ideas, values and norms of the society or institution of which they are a member. Credulous and zealous, eager to please their superiors and ardent to receive in turn recognition of their devotion, such persons would in a civilian context be merely silly, but in the context of armed combat they become – to those obliged to obey their orders – dangerous in the extreme.

Morgdahl talks and acts like a plucky, upright adolescent hero out of some naïve late nineteenth century dime novel. Coyly avoiding obscene and blasphemous oaths by means of expressions such as "cheese and crackers," taking pains to be clean-shaven even under combat conditions, appealing to what he mistakenly imagines must be his men's determination to be "game" or to live up to the ideal of a "good scout," Morgdahl is a mortal danger to his men. Anxious to impress Stollman, he performs his duties with undue zeal, exceeding the limits of his assigned missions and thereby unnecessarily placing his platoon in increased peril. His platoon loses nine men in only a week.

The ultimate pompous poseur of the entire Mechanized Cavalry Group is the recently arrived replacement, Lieutenant Simmons – known contemptuously to the men as Buffalo Bill by reason of the luxuriant moustache and goatee that he affects. Simmons is a smug prig imbued with illusions of heroism derived from Hollywood films. He is a strutting, sanctimonious narcissist, utterly insensible of and indifferent to the proprieties of combat soldiers and the exigencies of combat conditions. His arrogant, meddlesome behaviour on the front line inspires first defiance and later mutiny among the non-coms and the men, for the price of Simmons' self-delusions is their imperilment. It is ironic that Simmons becomes a fatal obstruction in the chain of command, for his is an ardent disciple and a willing tool of the Powell-Stollman alliance.

Among the enlisted men of the outfit only Corporal Finch embraces the kind of empty rhetoric and false ideals propagated by Powell and Stollman. Like Simmons, Finch has swallowed it all whole, taken up the heroic image as presented in books and films and made it his own. Finch was "suckered in ... they got to him when he was just a kid, that's the trouble with him." Similarly, of Finch's combat exploits, Riglioni observes: "his talent was that of an actor; so convinced he was a hero, he acted like one every time." Yet a vital difference between Finch and poseurs such as Morgdahl and Simmons is that Finch is truly skilful and useful in combat, and by acting out his illusions he endangers no-one else – to the contrary, he is an asset to the unit. Despite his dubious motivation and his vain desire to be decorated, Finch merits respect for his courage and initiative under fire. In the end, though, his pose is both fatal and futile – killed in action, Finch does not even posthumously receive the medal for which Riglioni recommended him, rather it is Stollman who is awarded the Silver Star for gallantry in action.

In opposition to the Powell-Stollman alliance and its stooges, there is – centered around Sal Riglioni and best represented by him – an affiliation of ordinary G.I.s whose only ambition is that of living through the war and returning to their homes, their families and their loved ones. Yet day after day, battle after battle, campaign after campaign, these frightened, lonely men carry out their hazardous duties, perform the perilous tasks they are assigned, striving to survive, to stay alive, but doing so without disregard for their fellows, without endangering or making unjust use of others to serve their own advantage.

Riglioni, the central figure of the novel, began the war burdened by the same kind of illusions which prove to be Finch's undoing. Crossing the ocean by troop ship en route to the war, Riglioni hoped for an attack on the ship by enemy planes so that he could perform acts of heroism that would win for him a decoration and make his father proud of him. But during the course of the campaigns he has fought in North Africa, in Normandy, through France and Belgium, and into Germany, Riglioni's naïve dreams of heroic deeds have been supplanted by a hopeless nausea and sickly horror. Now his most cherished desires are for gentle love and the priceless peace of ordinary life.

As the novel opens, with the unit fighting in the Rhineland, Riglioni is already suffering extreme mental fatigue. Apprehensive and full of dread, forced to confront death and horror day after day and night after night, he feels his mind going. Yet even as Riglioni becomes increasingly disordered and dissociated, hallucinating, withdrawing into fantasy and memory, he begins to attain a new clarity concerning his condition and to gain new insights into the system in which he is trapped, recognizing himself as "an ignorant cog in somebody else's wheel."

Punished by Stollman with extra missions for refusing to respect the authority of Lieutenant Simmons, witnessing the men in his unit crack up, become demented, get shot and blown up, one after another, Riglioni at last revolts against the system – the chain of command – and disengages himself from it. He resigns his sergeancy, busting himself to the rank of private, and refuses any longer to lead his men into combat. Ultimately, completely disgusted with and outraged by Captain Stollman's perfidy, Riglioni even refuses to follow orders except upon condition that Stollman personally lead the unit into battle. Riglioni is joined in his rebellion by the surviving enlisted members of "A" Troop.

Even when Riglioni is tempted by Stollman with a promise of promotion to First Sergeant, a rank that would remove him from the front line and admit him to the sanctuary of the command post, he contemptuously declines to rejoin the system. Riglioni's desperate integrity, united with his flight into fantasy – his hypnotic fascination with the light of Atman's candles – is a fateful combination, one that leads to the destruction both of himself and of "A" Troop when the rebellious, heedless unit is swiftly overrun in the unexpected German counter-offensive.

Yet futile and disastrous as it proves to be, Riglioni's rebellion represents an assertion of the highest qualities of the human spirit: an affirmation of the ideals of fairness and freedom, and a repudiation of selfishness and hypocrisy. In contrast to Riglioni's steadfast stance against corrupt authority, we see in the novel the capitulation of three of his long-suffering fellow soldiers, Muldoon, Enshaw and Proctor, each of whom concludes a bargain with Stollman. In return for the promise or even the possibility of safety and survival in the command post, each man consents to serve Stollman's interests, to speak for and to further the Captain's purposes among the men of the unit. Moreover, the three soldiers even sign the papers recommending Stollman for the Silver Star.

Another figure in the novel who undergoes a process of psychic development similar to that of Riglioni – and yet ultimately significantly different from him – is Private Paul Gingold. Gingold is a replacement who has been with the unit for about two months and has proven himself competent and reliable in combat, yet his true character remains something of a mystery to the others in the unit who have not yet been able to appraise him. As Riglioni observes of him: "Gingold was either a particularly unorthodox sort of wag or a complete idiot." The reason that Gingold is suspected of being the latter is a consequence of the obtuse expression that he frequently wears on his face. In fact, the expression is part of Gingold's strategy of secret, subtle resistance to the institution of the army and its hierarchy. He is, indeed, as Riglioni suspects, possessed of a dry, sly, satirical wit.

An early example in the novel of Gingold's deadpan pointed humour occurs when Colonel Powell –

making one his rare appearances in any proximity to the combat zone – is watching "A" Troop advance toward the front. Gingold in the turret of an armoured car passing the Colonel swings the .50 caliber machine gun into a vertical position in a parody of the "present arms" posture, in this manner mocking the Colonel but maintaining as he does so an expression of "irremediable stupidity." Nor, as the reader later learns, is this the first occasion on which Gingold has perpetrated this kind of private gesture of derision. It is a technique he perfected earlier in his army career when he made it a point to maintain an ingenuous mien as he deliberately saluted officers in theatre lobbies, latrines and other inappropriate locations. Although aggressive in combat, and as a Jew, a motivated opponent of Nazism, Gingold is at the same time engaged in a quiet artful revolt against the institution of the military.

Gingold becomes traumatized for a time by an incident that occurs during the quiet aftermath of a firefight: while engaged in executing a bowel movement in the concealment of a hedge, he is ambushed by a German soldier. Although fired upon at extremely close range by the German, Gingold miraculously escapes being wounded or killed. After an initial fit of emotional excitability immediately following the incident, Gingold withdraws into a state of shock and thereafter expresses himself only in terms of excremental epithets and metaphors. The impact of the ambush upon Gingold is to provoke a disordered psychic state in which he becomes obsessed with the notion that everything is "shit," that is to say that existence itself and all forms of human activity are base and vile.

Gingold remains for days in a state of semi-lunacy, "calling all creation a turd." But at length he recovers his wits in time to perceive the imminent peril in which "A" Troop by reason of its desperate insurgency has placed itself. Gingold remonstrates with Riglioni, attempting to make him see the futility of his position: "Don't cut off our nose to spite Stollman's face, Rig." Gingold attempts to rouse the other soldiers of the demoralized, rebellious "A" Troop who sit or recline in the cellar, lost in reverie, staring vacantly into the hypnotic flames of Atman's candles. At last, Gingold forcibly extinguishes the candles, breaking the spell. But although he succeeds in convincing Riglioni of the danger of their situation and in stirring him to take action, it is too late to take effective measures against the German attack, and the unit is annihilated.

Badly wounded during the final battle, Gingold is the sole survivor of "A" Troop. The novel ends with a sort of epilogue in the form of a letter, written by Gingold during his convalescence at a military hospital, addressed to Dr. Pennybaker, an army psychiatrist, who on behalf of Headquarters has been persistently questioning Gingold in order to discover the cause of the collapse of "A" Troop during the German counter-attack.

Gingold's letter serves to express the final phase of his psychic development. Having recovered from his temporary, shock-induced lunacy, and having subsequently recovered from a severe head wound received in the final devastating battle of "A" Troop, Gingold is confined to the psychiatric ward of an Army hospital. He is thought by the staff to be suffering from a mental disorder occasioned by his head wound, but he has, in fact, emerged from his traumatic combat experience with a new lucidity of mind and a new sense of identity.

The reason that Gingold is thought to be mentally unsound is that he has consistently refused either to identify himself (having in order to avoid persecution or execution as a jew in the event of capture thrown away his dog-tags after his wounding) or to answer any of the questions put to him concerning the cause of "A" Troop's annihilation. But Gingold's grounds for so acting are eminently sane; his refusal represents an act of rebellion against definitions of identity and reality that are wholly unacceptable to him. (Shades of Herman Melville's "Bartleby.") Gingold declines any longer to co-operate with the institution that helped to destroy his friends. He refuses to lend any further support to the reductive concepts of reality by which the institution functions and justifies itself.

Gingold has learned that the world is not "shit" – as during his temporary lunacy he believed it to be – but rather that it is defiled by the presence upon it of hypocritical, sanctimonious, egotistical despots of all degrees and descriptions who strive to wield power over others. The mode of resistance against such moral contamination of the world that Gingold has chosen is that of non-cooperation and of subtle, determined subversion: he will neither play their game nor speak their language, he will puncture their complacency with irony and mockery, he will learn to recognize and resist those tendencies within himself that might ally him with institutions and their parasitical potentates, he will evade the machinations of "fakes and clowns," and will survive to live the full life of a free and independent human, loving a woman and breeding children.

Apart from, but related to, the two conflicting configurations of characters that constitute the moral poles of *The Wax Boom,* there are two figures – Lieutenant Spiro and Ken Atman – who embody in their purest form opposite alternatives of outlook and conduct.

Lieutenant Spiro represents in the novel the possibility of leadership exercised for the common good, authority without egotism, ideals and values without cant. Spiro is a highly competent, effective combat officer whose terseness and directness of speech are in marked contrast to the bluster of Colonel Powell and Lieutenant Simmons and the self-justifications and manipulatory glibness of Captain Stollman. Spiro is quietly practical and unassuming, inspiring in the men of his platoon respect and affection, who think of him as "a magic bulldog who kept his men alive somehow."

In contrast to the somber sense of moral obligation that characterizes Lieutenant Spiro, Private Ken Atman embodies a spirit of cynicism and disruption, iconoclasm and rebellion. A recent replacement, only a week or so on the front line, Atman exerts a powerful, baleful influence on "A" Troop. It is he who causes the wax boom of the novel's title, with his discovery that the numerous statues of Christ and of the saints which are to be found in the churches and homes of the small German towns in which "A" Troop is engaged, are formed of wax – wax from which candles can be made. Atman – an iconoclast in both a literal and figurative sense – has no compunction about destroying these religious icons, and his lack of reverence soon inspires similar behaviour in other members of "A" Troop.

The sudden abundance of candles among the men has the effect of causing them (like Tennyson's "Lotus Eaters") to withdraw into reverie and fantasy, forsaking their duties for the hypnotic visions of the candle flames. Atman's wax boom, together with the subtle influence of his irreverent, anarchic spirit, thus plays a vital role in catalyzing the insurgency of "A" Troop.

Ultimately, Atman is an ambiguous, enigmatic figure. Though, like Gingold, he embodies the spirit of mockery and rebellion, he soon comes to assume the position of "a big shot in the outfit, like a religious leader," even enshrining himself upon a kind of self-constructed alter, composed of seven mattresses piled one atop the other, flanked by candles nine feet high. There is certainly a disturbing contradiction in the speed and ease with which the iconoclast comes himself to achieve the status and power of an institution. Moreover, there is something of a facile and shallow quality about Atman's nihilism – not only does it fail to distinguish between degrees of institutional oppression (the Nazis versus the U.S. Army) but ultimately it shows itself to be a futile and destructive influence as "A" Troop is destroyed as a consequence of its passive rebellion.

Atman's name suggests, of course, the Hindu word for the human soul or spirit, but this would seem to be ironic, since, as noted, he is utterly lacking in any religious feeling, callously smashing with his rifle butt the wax figure of a crucified Christ, and further mocking religion with coloured pictures of Christ – impudently and blasphemously inscribed to himself – which he tapes up in various locations.

Atman's manner is such that it is difficult to know if he is genuinely ingenuous or if his seeming naïve simplicity is a part of an elaborate ironic pose. Perhaps the final word on this mysterious figure is the refrain that runs through Gingold's mind while he is in the psychiatric ward: "Who is Atman, what is he?"

In *The Wax Boom,* the war serves to disclose and illuminate another war – that of the institution versus the individual. A dominant theme of the book is the predicament of men trapped in an organization that victimizes and destroys them. The army is only one instance, one aspect of the organized egotism that can be named as the institution. The institution embraces political, economic and cultural life. The grade school principal, the congressman, the university academics and their student imitators, the boss who degrades and exploits his workers – all these are depicted in the novel as serving the institution, all of them further the process by which human beings are "trained to feed on crumbs, trained to feed on each other."

Language is seen in the novel as a primary tool of the institution, language that obscures the truth: the affected martial obscenity of Colonel Powell, the clichéd, hackneyed speech of Lieutenant Simmons; the glib, manipulative phrases of Captain Stollman; the smug, reductive pronouncements of Dr. Pennybaker, the army psychiatrist; the deceptive, distortive language of newspapers and magazines and radio broadcasts; the mendacious language of advertising. The institution is served by words that dupe and delude, and by ranks and titles that maintain the hierarchy of masters and men.

Related to the abuse of language by figures in the novel associated with the institution is the improper use to which personal names are put. Lieutenant Simmons addresses the individual soldiers of "A" Troop by their rank rather than their names, thus denying them an identity apart from their lives as soldiers, their functions in the institution. Captain Stollman employs an opposite device, calling his subordinates by their first names in order to imply an intimacy, an amicability and a solicitude for them that will serve to conceal his callous use of them. Captain Churney does likewise, memorizing for purposes of manipulation the name of every soldier in the entire Mechanized Cavalry Group. Colonel Powell, on the other hand, is so self-important that he fails at first to recognize Gingold's name as being a name at all, and then dismisses it contemptuously: "Gingold? What kind of ignorant name is that?"

Significantly, by the end of the novel, Gingold has learned to withhold his name, inventing a series of preposterous aliases, thus denying the institution any further leverage on his life. By refusing to identify himself by name, Gingold resists being classified and categorized by the institution of the military. By so simple a device does he evade their control. Gingold's namelessness is, in fact, an assertion of his personal uniqueness, a defense of his selfhood, his autonomy, his individuality. Similarly, by refusing to reply to the questions posed to him by Dr. Pennybaker, Gingold rejects the narrow conceptual system of which the psychiatrist's queries are the expression. Gingold will neither be defined by nor permit his experiences to be interpreted according to the shallow abstractions of the institution.

The central issue of *The Wax Boom* is the question of resistance to the system, the organization, to the social and political power structures, the constituted authorities and their processing, their programming, their control of human lives. In the novel, the ultimate stakes of the conflict between individual humans and the institution are shown to be high, indeed. Beyond the prospect of physical annihilation faced by the soldiers, there is the moral death attendant upon collaboration with the institution. And ultimately, upon the outcome of the conflict between the individual and the institution depends the fate of the human race, whether humans will shape their institutions or be shaped by them and then face "the long dull dying of the race in shrouds of hypocrisy, in cobwebs of insipidity." For apart from the war between nations, the deadly struggle against the enemy, there is the other, more subtle war, the other enemy: the identity-obliterating institution and its agents. Sal Riglioni perceives the insidious two-front war in which he and his fellow soldiers are engaged – "a man knew that his destiny was turned by madmen and fools" – but his outright rebellion against the institution proves vain and self-destructive. Gingold also realizes the dual character of the war and the enemy, railing against "the outlandish way in which we let fakes and clowns bleed us to death," but his is a more far-sighted strategy of resistance, taking the form of evasion and disengagement.

Both Riglioni and Gingold understand that the war against the institution is not a simple us-against-them conflict, but rather that the battles must be fought and won and fought again and again in each human conscience. The temptation to be safe, to be comfortable at the expense of your fellows is one that must be defeated over and over again. Riglioni sees reliable men such as Proctor and Enshaw defect at last to the institution, and he recognizes that "the self you learned to cherish turned suddenly as inhuman as the captain who taught you contempt for all the brothers who might have saved you along with the race." Riglioni sees too that the "super-realists," the callous egotists who serve and who thrive in the institution are really no more than men who have surrendered to what is most ignoble in themselves, the same vain egotism and base selfishness in every human heart: "it was the little bit of them in every man that added up to all the Buffalo Bills and Stollmans and Colonels like Powell."

Similarly, Gingold in his passionate written castigation of all the arrogance, hypocrisy, sanctimony and vicious superficiality that characterize the world of the established order, reflects that "the sins and faults and failings which repel us so in others are those that exist to the most revolting degrees in ourselves."

At issue in *The Wax Boom* is the necessity for rebellion against dehumanizing institutions and imposed constructs versus the perils inherent in such rebellion. Atman may be seen to represent one such innate peril, that of an indiscriminate, habitual, predictable opposition to authority and structure which itself then assumes the status of a dogma and an imperative, and which thus tends ultimately to end in a new kind of control and command structure. One extreme, futile form of rebellion is represented in the novel by the figure of Scarbro, a battle-fatigued G.I. whose unconscious mind ultimately rebels against the unendurable, enforced horror of his existence by causing him to forget the meanings of the simplest words and concepts, thus rendering him completely ineffective as a soldier, but at the same time impairing him greatly as a human being. Another desperate, self-defeating form of rebellion is that undertaken by Riglioni and his associates, a passive withdrawal into fantasy, a vain denial of external danger, a tactic which proves in the end to be fatal. The most promising form of rebellion in the novel is that enacted by Gingold – a considered, reflective, determined resistance that is as appropriate to peacetime conditions as to the conditions of war. Gingold's strategy of revolt derives from his perception that the institution and rebellion against it are like a Scylla and a Charybdis – both too much control and too little control are forms of tyranny, both manipulation and anarchy are ultimately destructive of independence and identity.

In its sharp, intense, hallucinated depiction of combat, in its vivid delineation of the dark and raw minds of fighting men, in the purity of its rage and pathos, and the acuteness of its moral vision, *The Wax Boom* is among the few finest American novels of World War II. And yet I have never seen the novel discussed or even mentioned in critical studies of the literature of the Second World War. Somehow, the book seems to have passed unnoticed.

One reason, I believe, that such a noteworthy novel as *The Wax Boom* has not received due recognition is that it appeared at an inopportune time, when interest in World War II was flagging, after the market had been satiated if not saturated. At the time of its publication in 1962, Mandel's novel attracted little attention and following the publication of the novel in a paperback format in 1963, no subsequent editions have been undertaken.

The sad fate of *The Wax Boom* makes poignant a contemporaneous review from the *Indianapolis Star* cited on the back cover of the paperback edition of the book: "The perspective of years will single it out as one of the truly marvellous creations of our era."

The Wax Boom was George Mandel's fourth novel, preceded by *Flee the Angry Strangers* (1952), *The Breakwater* (1960), and *Into the Woods of the World* (1961.) For a time during the late 1950s and early 1960s, the author's writing was associated with the literature of the Beat Generation. An early short story by Mandel, "The Beckoning Sea," was included in the anthology, *The Beat Generation and the Angry Young Men* (1958) edited by Gene Feldman and Max Gartenberg. Mandel's fiction is cited and repeatedly singled out for praise in Lawrence Lipton's study of the tastes and mores of the Beat

Generation, *The Holy Barbarians* (1959.) Lipton characterizes Mandel's work as being "popular in beat generation circles for what he says as well as for the way he says it." Ultimately, though, Mandel is far too much his own man even to be included among that diverse and quirky fellowship known as the Beats. There is in his work an essential quality of unlikeness and sovereignty.

The critical neglect of George Mandel's writing is to me a matter of continuing astonishment and disappointment. He possesses rare and vital gifts as a writer – originality, insight, wit and imagination – yet all of his angry, funny, rich and complex books, which should by now have found a permanent place in postwar American literature, have for a very long time been and at present remain out of print.

The Wax Boom by George Mandel, New York, Random House, 1962. Reprinted in paperback format by Bantam Books, New York, 1963.

LAWLESS LOVE:
A Prison, A Paradise

"Without Contraries is no progression," wrote William Blake in *The Marriage of Heaven and Hell.* "Attraction & Repulsion, Reason & Energy, Love & Hate," Blake expounded, "are necessary to Human existence." Loran Hurnscot, the author of *A Prison, A Paradise* and an avowed admirer of Blake's writings, would, I think, concur in that proposition. Indeed, interpenetrating contraries and spiritual progression comprise the central theme of this unusual book.

A Prison, A Paradise, published in London in 1958, consists of excerpts selected by the author from her personal journals and daily diaries. The first journal entry is dated November 3, 1922 and the final entry is dated February 20, 1958 (or shortly before publication of the book.) At one point, in early 1929, the journals break off, then resume in May of 1936. This hiatus marks a division of focus and subject matter corresponding to the book's separation into two numbered and titled sectons, "Volume One, The Summer Birdcage" and "Volume Two, The Tilted Spiral." The two separate volumes that make up *A Prison, A Paradise* are each furnished with a frontispiece in the form of an engraved illustration taken from the 1845 edition of Thomas Quarles *Emblems, Divine and Moral.* These engravings serve to encapsulate the dominant theme of each volume.

The first emblem, preceding Volume One, depicts a female figure confined in a cage, the structure of which resembles a birdcage. As the prisoner looks out through the bars of her enclosure, she holds hands with an angel who kneels beside the cage. The illustration may be seen to express in a single image the events of the first volume, the author's sense of imprisonment in an unhappy marriage and in an obsessive, futile love affair, together with the intimations she sometimes receives of a transcendent reality. The second emblem, preceding Volume Two, portrays a female figure sitting on the earth, her arms outstretched in welcome or worship, her face turned to a beam of sunlight that shines full upon her. Behind the seated figure is a circle of shadow or perhaps a hole out of which she has climbed. Near the top of the illustration is a representation of the sun on which in Hebrew letters, the Tetragrammaton or name of God is written. God's holy sunlight has dispelled a ring of dark cloud in the sky and warms and illuminates the grateful, reverent figure seated on the earth. This illustration can be seen to serve as a metaphor for the authors experience in later life of a sense of divine rescue and blessedness, and of her turning her attention away from the things of earth and toward God.

Hurnscot begins to keep her journal at a time of crisis in her life, amid the tensions and turmoil occasioned by a love-triangle. As readers, we are thus plunged into the thick of things, compelled to seize upon clues and comments to make sense of events, ignorant of the personal histories that serve to motivate the principals involved in the unfolding account. Only piecemeal does a systematic narrative emerge. This approach is, of course, dramatically effective, a form of delayed decoding that engages and maintains reader interest. In the following, though, for the sake of clarity, I will set forth in chronological order the circumstances and incidents that comprise the narrative recorded in the first half of *A Prison, A Paradise.*

The first ward of Loran Hurnscot's invisible prison was her childhood home, presided over by her strange, sadistic mother. Based on Hurnscot's account of her unhappy childhood, it seems likely that her mother was in some way deranged. Her mother inflicted upon her not only blows and beatings but barbed insults, as well as playing cruel pranks such as taking her small daughter on long walks into the countryside, explaining to the girl that she was to be abandoned there to fend for herself. With craft and cunning, her mother was able to conceal such abuse from Loran's father, a vague, naïve man, absent-minded and often absent from home for long periods in pursuit of his profession. Hurnscot characterizes her childhood as one of fear and oppression.

Perhaps not unsurprisingly, already as an eight year old she finds herself entertaining thoughts of suicide. Promising deliverance from her wretched situation, the notion is profoundly attractive to her. "I hadn't known," she writes, "that there could be any escape from the, not daily and hourly, but *eternal* misery of living in the same house as an inwardly frantic woman, and the thought lay like a magic ring in my pocket. Sometimes it became quite obsessive ... ."

The second ward of Loran Hurnscot's personal, portable prison is her marriage to Hubert Tindall. Having escaped the cold cruelty of her mother, Loran rather impetuously enters into marriage with a man with whom she has been acquainted for a period of less than three months. As an adolescent, Hubert suffered from tuberculosis, a circumstance that caused him to be schooled at home and treated indulgently by his family. As a man, he seems to Loran to be lively, charming and intelligent, but after their marriage he soon reveals a side to his character that is petulant, demanding and tyrannical. And following a few unfortunate attempts at sexual intimacy with his bride, he forever foregoes any further erotic attentions to her. (Loran later concludes – on the basis of this and other evidence – that her husband is a repressed homosexual.) In the course of two years of marriage, during which they live very frugally while labouring long hours to operate a small press, Hubert becomes a sullen, selfish bully. Meanwhile, his T.B. has again become active. Only out of loyalty and pity does Loran remain with him.

The very dungeon of the author's psychic incarceration is her highly volatile and ultimately ruinous love affair with Barny, an author, married but irremediably promiscuous. What seems to Loran to be an opportunity to break free of the misery of her loveless marriage proves to be a trap: a "temporary and delusive heaven." It is Hubert, her husband, who encourages her to find a lover. Indeed, he insists upon it and mocks and insults her when she is slow to do so. When, however, she commences an amorous liaison with Barny, Hubert quickly becomes jealous and angry. His bullying and violent rages reach new heights until his conduct becomes insupportable and they separate. Loran's relation to Barny is one of lawless, boundless passion. It is, she writes, "like possession by a demon." She becomes obsessed with him and addicted to their ardent erotic encounters, a "prisoner of love," as the phrase goes. Intermittently, their relationship is "heavenly," a "paradise," but Barny is compulsively faithless. He desires and pursues sexual activity with various women simultaneously. Early enchantment and delicious sensuality soon turn to bitter acrimony. The two quarrel and wound each other. Repeatedly, they part and make-up. The reader soon loses count of the number of times that they terminate their fraught relationship only to recommence it again. Loran comes to feel such despair and grief of heart that she attempts suicide. She aborts Barny's child. She flees abroad but upon her return again resumes their relationship. By their final, definitive parting – after a two year clash of flesh and will with her demon lover – Loran feels debased and ashamed, broken and drained, battered and empty. In the meantime, Hubert's revived tuberculosis puts an end to his life. During his final days, Loran and Hubert are reconciled but not before Hubert – in a last vengeful gesture – has disinherited her. With her husband's death and the end of her affair with Barny, Loran is, at last, free of both her male jailers, the "cold bully" and the "cold lecher," but the ordeals she has endured have left her desolate and disconsolate.

Occurring at intervals among the emotional convulsions chronicled in the diaries of Volume One are entries regarding incidents that can be seen to prefigure the dramatic interior transformation that takes place in Volume Two. From early childhood, Loran conceives, as she relates, a dislike of conventional, institutional religion, later in adult life forsaking all interest in spiritual matters, instead, devoting her attention to political questions and to art, music and literature. On one occasion, though, in conversation with a friend, she records that the topic is that of "immortality and why one hoped there was a meaning in things." Some time later, having a tooth extracted by a dentist, under the influence of nitrous oxide, Loran experiences what she regards as a revelation: "Saw God, and knew that the soul was immortal, and all truths one." (The author is not alone in having had a vision of this nature. See, for example, Benjamin Bloods *The Anaesthetic Revelation and the Gist of Philosophy,* 1874, and *An Ether Vision* by Frederick Hall in *The Open Court,* 1909.) When she visits and tends to her dying husband, she tells him of her vision of "an absolute truth that comprehended all facets of truth in time," and her sense that after bodily death, there is "continuance." Although at this troubled and tormented time of her life, her vision does little to assuage the pain and exhaustion she feels, it may be seen as a small seed slowly germinating in her spirit.

This small seed is further nourished by two incidents. Loran becomes seriously ill and must undergo an emergency operation, during which – under the influence of the anaesthetic – she again experiences a cosmic vision. Afterward, she writes: "Something changed, the night of the operation. I know I came back *different*. ... I had what I was in such desperate need of – *help from the outside.*" There is also a strange occurrence one evening some months after Hubert's death when with a friend she attends an intimate dinner party. The hostess insists on reading the palms of her two guests. Loran is inwardly scornful of the woman and her purported abilities, even though her friend insists that the woman knows things she cannot possibly know. When Loran reluctantly agrees to have her palm read, the woman soon enters into a state of trance-like possession and begins to weep and sob. In great distress she tells Loran that her weeping comes from "him," *he* (clearly Hubert's spirit) never meant her to be unhappy: "he wants you to know that he never meant it to be like this – it's all gone wrong, it isn't what he meant, he wants you to be happy – he won't go, he won't leave me till you really know it isn't what he meant." Shaken by the experience, Loran reflects that if she accepts as true what has just transpired then "a life after death is certain."

A central component of Loran Hurnscot's character, serving as a connection or conductor between sensuality and spirituality is her intense response to natural beauty. Throughout the diaries she is alert and alive to every aspect of the world of nature: trees and flowers, reeds and moss, rivers and ponds, clouds and birdsong, fragrances, soughing winds and purling water, subtleties of light and color, the changing moon and the moving stars. It is clear from her descriptions that she possesses extensive and precise knowledge of such things and that she delights in them. Implicit in her intimate psychological link to the natural world is a pantheistic sense of the presence there of a living spirit. It is significant that on the two occasions when she attempts suicide, she chooses to enter a river, as if seeking to resolve her unendurable particularity in an eternal and unitary force.

The "tilted spiral" to which the title of Volume Two of *A Prison, A Paradise* alludes is the author's metaphor for describing the shape of spiritual growth, as she has experienced it. The spiritual life, she writes, is "full of false starts, false scents, false dawns." Nor is spiritual progress consistent or continuous. "One labours," she laments, "lumbers up the hard hard slope ... and in no time at all one is sliding down again." There are, moreover, a bewildering number of paths to pick and of guides to follow, some better suited than others to the purpose. And yet, ascent of the interior spiral is the final and paramount end of human existence. God is (as Kenneth Burke has written somewhere) at once our goal and our goad.

If in Volume One, the authors prison was an unhappy marriage and her paradise sexual love (soon proving itself to be equally a prison) then in Volume Two, the image of prison is expanded to suggest the spirit's hapless embodiment in the temporal, material world, while the image of paradise is extended to designate that blessed, blissful state in which the spirit is granted communion with "the true, the radiant world" of Divinity.

The pivotal event in Loran's life occurs during her second attempt at suicide. Her first attempt at self-destruction took place during her painful "imprisonment" in relations with her cruel husband, Hubert, and her callous, faithless lover, Barney. On that occasion, Loran tried to drown herself in a river, but the animal spirit within her refused to be annihilated. Her body would not obey her repeated efforts to dive deep and remain below the water. A decade later, driven less by a particular misery than by a general despair (and a life-long, deep-seated attraction to death) Loran prepares her second suicide attempt with calm, meticulous deliberation. She makes a will, withdraws from the bank her few remaining pounds, and travels by train to a previously chosen spot: "a river that never gave up its dead." Her plan is to take several sleeping pills and then on the edge of unconsciousness, allow herself to fall into the river.

Arriving at last at the banks of the river and having waited patiently for dusk, when the last visitors to the river depart, she is prevented from her dark purpose by an urgent and potent realization: "It came over me, blindingly, for the first time in my life, that suicide was a wrong act, was indeed 'mortal sin.' In that moment God stopped me. I did not want my life, but I knew I was suddenly forbidden by something outside myself to let it go. ... A tremendous 'NO' rose – within me? outside me? I don't know. ... There was no earthly help for me anywhere, but I knew I was no longer alone; that God was there. It had always been pride that had held me off from Him. Now it was broken the obstacle was gone."

This victorious confrontation with a profound and powerful inward urge to self-destruction serves to catalyze within the author a process of psychic re-orientation. It removes from her mind the secret suicide-obsession she has nourished since childhood and – like a compass needle pointing north – aligns her spirit toward the Divine. About one month after this harrowing yet happy transformation, while walking alone in the countryside one sunny autumn day, Loran undergoes a further spiritual awakening. First noting in her journal the utter insufficiency of her description of the event, she writes: "suddenly I was swept out of myself – knowing, knowing, knowing. Feeling the love of God burning through creation, and an ecstasy of bliss pouring through my spirit and down into every nerve."

During the years that follow, experiences of a similar nature occur: blessedness, radiance, ecstasy, transfiguration. In the manner almost of a secular nun, Loran lives a frugal, humble life, much given to prayer, contemplation and little acts of kindness and sympathy. Her spiritual convictions remain decidedly non-dogmatic, non-denominational. Drawn in equal measure to Christianity and to Eastern religions, she would like, she writes, to effect a marriage of East and West. As her earlier erotic passion was outside laws and codes, so, too, now is her spiritual life: "I have what could only be called a lawless love of God."

One of Loran's chief pleasures during this second phase of her life is the opportunity to encounter a wide variety of human lives. Her ill-paid and intermittent employment as an interviewer obliges her to travel a good deal within the United Kingdom and affords her opportunities to meet many sorts and conditions of humankind. She very much cherishes the sincerity, eccentricities and wisdom of the ordinary people with whom her job brings her into contact, recording in her journal incidents, conversations and anecdotes, seeing in the myriad of lives and fates embodiments of vital lessons. She also reads extensively on spiritual matters, perusing the work of visionary poets such as Thomas Traherne and William Blake, and studying Plotinus, Meister Eckhart, Julian of Norwich, Jacob Boehme, Saint Teresa, Swedenborg, Pascal, Kierkegaard, Jung, Vedanta, the Tao te Ching, *The Secret of the Golden Flower*, George Bernanos, Nikolaj Berdayev, Simone Weil and Thomas Merton. She possesses an independent mind and a critical intelligence, gratefully garnering insights from others, but rejecting what she finds to be not in accordance with her own experience or in consonance with her own heart. Ouspensky, for example, she dismisses as "too cold and too shallow." She is also sceptical of political ideologies and ideologues, doctrines and movements.

It is also noteworthy, I think, that – like William Blake whom she admires – Loran does not view the erotic aspect of the human make-up as base or sinful but rather as a potential vehicle of spiritual experience. Eventually, she comes to see her sufferings with Hubert and Barney as preparing the ground for her mystical experiences. In this way, she is able to forgive and to pray for her persecutors. In all of this, there is no trace of self-satisfaction or false humility. Hurnscot writes candidly of her lapses and what she views as her foolishness, her weakness and incompetence. Her journal concludes with a determination to continue to pursue her quiet spiritual self-refinement with the goal of uprooting from her mind "the black tentacled thing" that is the ego.

Loran Hurnscot was a pseudonym invented by the author, Gay Taylor (1896-1970.) Gay Taylor was, in turn, a pseudonym used by Ethelwynne Stewart McDowall, who in 1920 married Harold Taylor, with whom she founded the Golden Cockrell Press. Under the name Gay Taylor, she was the author of a novel titled *No Goodness in the Worm* (London, 1930) which I have not read, but which would seem to be a fictionalized version of the catastrophic love-triangle described in Volume One of *A Prison, a Paradise*. In *The Land Unknown* (London & New York, 1975) the second volume of an autobiography by the poet, Kathleen Raine, several pages are devoted to an account of Raine's friendship with Gay Taylor. Raine begins by stating that "Of all the friends of a lifetime, in retrospect I understand, Gay was one of the most remarkable as well as one of the most loved." She praises Gay for her humour, her curiosity about life, her "perfect truthfulness," and her practice of praying for strangers which was the true "work of her life." Raine states that the name Loran Hurnscot is an anagram of what Gay Taylor saw as "her two besetting sins, sloth and rancour." Raine remarks that, in fact, no one could have been less slothful or less rancorous than her friend.

Candid, vivid and thoughtful, as a modern spiritual autobiography *A Prison, A Paradise* bears comparison to Thomas Merton's *The Seven Storey Mountain* (1948) though through their respective explorations, contemplations and epiphanies the two authors reach different conclusions with regard to traditional Christian beliefs and the utility of religious institutions. (Admirable as is Loran Hurnscot's independence of mind, her insistent, categorical dismissal of Church dogma and discipline is itself parochial. Surely, climbers may approach the top of the mountain from any side.) Readers engaged with spiritual themes will find this a work of permanent interest and value.

A Prison, A Paradise
by Loran Hurnscot
Vicor Gollancz Ltd. London,
and Viking Press, New York, 1958

NOUGHT IS NULLED:
The Hole in the Zero

"Nobody present here which was not there before.
Only is order othered. Nought is nulled."
Finnegans Wake

As an imaginative representation of what it means to be human under the aspect of eternity, to be caught between cosmos and chaos, between chance and fate, between wonder and terror, I know of few works of fiction that make so marked an impression on the mind of the reader or linger so vividly in the memory as M.K. Joseph's strange and striking novel, *The Hole in the Zero.* (1967.)

Set in a distant future, *The Hole in the Zero* treats of the primal perennial themes of human identity, the nature of the real, and the power of the imagination. The metaphysical vision that informs the novel is eclectically compounded of elements drawn from Neoplatonism, alchemy, hermetic philosophy, and Romanticism.

Briefly told, the novel concerns the fate of four characters who in a specially equipped spaceship undertake a journey beyond the boundaries of the vast spatio-temporal universe into the realm of "unspace, untime, unlaw, unpossibility". A deliberate act of sabotage vindictively committed by one of the four leaves them all stranded in the void without hope of rescue or return, utterly helpless except for the latent power of their minds to conceive and sustain identities and realities. Subject to the random probabilities and radical instabilities of the void, the four figures pass through a series of transformations in continually shifting scenes, enacting – as in a dream – parts in which their essential characters are revealed, realised and, in some cases, refined.

The four characters are Kraag, a cosmic tycoon; Kraag's daughter, Helena; Hyperion Merganser, who is Kraag's stooge and official heir-executive, as well as being the contracted fiancé of Kraag's daughter; and Seth Paradine, a Limitary Warden – that is a member of a corps of trained specialists who monitor the behaviour of the void in order to warn against its advance.

Following the immobilisation of all the power sources of their spacecraft, the four humans begin to be subject to the capricious and unpredictable un-laws of the void, where nothing and everything is possible, including random temporary probabilities, tentative patterns that form and dissolve in an instant or an eternity of time. At first the four are utterly lost, forsaken, defenceless and dispossessed in the anti-universe in which they are marooned, but gradually their separate consciousnesses begin to interact with the void, and forgetting their previous identities and experiences, they live in worlds created by their fears and desires. These worlds are revelatory of the deepest traits of their characters, reflections of the essential qualities of their minds.

The Hole in the Zero seems to me essentially to be a kind of Neoplatonic allegory of self-refinement, self-realisation, and self-transcendence. The four characters may be seen as figures embodying varying modes of awareness or levels of consciousness.

The lowest, most primitive state of mind is that personified by Kraag, who – as his name suggests – represents the earth-bound, the cloddish, that which is lacking in spirit and animation. Dull and unimaginative, but single-minded and ruthlessly determined, Kraag seeks nourishment in possessions and power. His is the level of gross materialism and moral blindness. Significantly, in his various incarnations Kraag appears as a blind feeder; a carved stone statue whose "thwarted, violent, blind life" rages imprisoned within it; and finally as a massive mountain veiled by cloud, insensible, inert, which then in an instant is dispersed as insubstantial, a mere illusion.

Merganser embodies a state of consciousness very much akin to but slightly superior to that of Kraag. Like Kraag he is aggressive and self-asserting, but rather than pursuing power and possessions, Merganser's appetite is for pleasure. His is the level of amoral, selfish hedonism. His surname is that of a fish-eating, diving bird with a slender bill. Together with his forename, "Bill", Merganser's names suggest his predacious character and his penchant for descent. His boyhood nickname, "Hippo", suggests both his large size and great strength, together with his animal nature. The significance of

Merganser's legal name, "Hyperion", I shall discuss later in another connection, but clearly it is intended to disguise his true character in the same manner that his expensive clothes and extensive plastic surgery are attempts to conceal from others his real nature.

Indeed, duplicity is Merganser's most distinguishing quality – his polished and urbane manner serving to dissemble his relentless, insatiable appetite for sensual gratification. The one undisguisable feature of Merganser's appearance is, however, his deficient pigmentation, his milk-white skin, his colourless hair, his red eyes. These physical characteristics are outward signs of Merganser's inward deficiencies, his lack of ethical principles or values.

The two remaining central characters of the novel – Helena and Paradine – may be seen as contrasting counterparts to the two foregoing figures, corresponding opposites to Kraag and Merganser respectively. For where Kraag represents the darkness of matter, the dullness of earth, Helena comes to represent matter in its alchemically highest and most refined state: gold. She becomes the golden woman, embodiment of the wisdom of the earth and of the body, priestess and prophetess of the One. Helen, as her name suggests, also embodies the aesthetic principle, Beauty, twin principle of the Truth. Not only is she herself beautiful, but she affirms beauty in all its forms, both in art and in nature.

Paradine is the contrasting counterpart to Merganser; thus their rivalry and mutual opposition in sequence after sequence of the novel, cycle after cycle of the void. Whereas Merganser's simple and exclusive aim in life is his personal pleasure, in pursuit of which he employs his imagination and will, Paradine possesses values and ideals that transcend the personal, exemplifying standards of service and responsibility. Accordingly, Paradine's imagination is employed by him not for personal fulfilment but in the understanding and admiration of beauty as it is expressed both in art and the natural world.

Paradine embodies in the novel the principles of ethics and order, and personifies also the highest function of human consciousness – the creative imagination. At the outset of the novel, Paradine distinguishes himself from the other figures not only by his dedication to a humane ideal – his service in the Limitary Authority, protecting colonies on the fringes of the universe – but also by having retained a childlike capacity for "make-believe", as he phrases it. By the end of the novel, after defending art, beauty and order in half-a-dozen different dream-worlds, Paradine has honed his will and enhanced his imaginative potentiality to the degree that he achieves communion with the creative power of the cosmos – a force immanent everywhere in the universe and latent in every mind – and creates "a new heaven and a new earth," renewing the universe and initiating a new cosmic cycle.

The allegorical significance of Paradine's name seems multi-valent. The prefix "para" means "beyond"; thus the name Para-dine may suggest one who is beyond feeding, beyond the base appetites that motivate Kraag and Merganser. Or, if this interpretation seems strained, the name may be seen to suggest the sound of the words "paradigm" and "paradise". These word associations would seem to be apt since Paradine possesses strong instincts for creating order or pattern, and since at the end of the novel he creates and inhabits a new paradise. Perhaps the word "paladin", a champion or outstanding protagonist of a cause, is also suggested by his Portmanteau name.

The Hole in the Zero is, as I have stated above, essentially Neoplatonic in its vision of the nature of reality and of the redemptive role of the creative imagination. The novel presents a universe in which there are a plurality of levels of being, the lowest of which is the material realm, the spatiotemporal world of separateness and selfishness; whereas the highest level is that of the One, the ultimate, unitive, creative principle from which all reality proceeds. The final goal of the human spirit is to liberate itself from materiality and to achieve mystical union with the One. But in its endeavour to emancipate itself the spirit is hindered by the lower nature of the animal body in which it is confined and by which its perception and consciousness are restricted.

Since the universe proceeds from the eternal creative act of the One, imagination is the true ground of being and the medium of all realities. Imagination is thus of paramount importance to the process of human spiritual liberation, serving as a vehicle of humanity's communion with the spiritual essence of reality.

Clearly, there are also affinities between M.K. Joseph's conception of the creative imagination and that shared by certain of the English romantic poets (who derived, of course, much inspiration from Neoplatonism.)

I am thinking in this regard of S.T. Coleridge's view of creative perception or imagination as "a repetition in the finite mind of the eternal act of creation in the infinite I AM." (*Biographia Literaria*.) Similarly, in *A Vision of the Last Judgement* William Blake maintained that only the transfiguring power of the imagination could redeem humanity from its condition of psychic fragmentation and ontological alienation:

"The Nature of my Work is Visionary or Imaginative; it is an Endeavour to restore what the Ancients have called the Golden Age.... This world of imagination is the World of Eternity, it is the Divine Bosom into which we shall all go after the death of the Vegetated Body. This World of Imagination is Infinite & Eternal, whereas The World of Generation or Vegetation, is Finite & for a small moment Temporal."

In *The Hole in the Zero,* the refinement and regeneration of the human spirit are symbolised in the final demise of Kraag and Merganser, and in the incremental acquisition of imaginative perception and creative power by Helena and Paradine, in whom beauty and wisdom, ethics and imagination ultimately are united.

The structure of the novel is essentially that of the archetypical Night Journey, the descent into chaos and darkness from which the traveller at length emerges purified, regenerated and enriched by new insight. Accordingly, order and disorder, death and rebirth are recurrent motifs in the text, culminating in Paradine's final reduction in mind and spirit to a condition of absolute zero immediately preceding his discovery of his latent creative potential, his power to imagine into being a new world.

Another implicit metaphorical structure in the narrative is that of the alchemical process, according to which metal (symbolising the human soul) can be perfected or healed by "killing" it and "reviving" it in a finer form. In this regard, it is significant that during one sequence in the novel Paradine appears as an alchemist, perhaps (as his name may also be seen to suggest) a parallel to the renown alchemist Paracelsus (1493-1541) who wrote that: "He who is born in imagination discovers the latent forces of Nature. ... Besides the stars that are established, there is yet another – *Imagination* that begets a new star and a new heaven." (*The Hermetic and Alchemical Writings of Parcelsus*, Vol. II, London: 1894.)

If *The Hole in the Zero* may be seen to proffer a kind cosmic myth, then the myth is also in large measure a comic one. Puns, jests, pastiche and light-hearted literary allusions abound in the text, serving both to counterpoint and to enhance the more dramatic and dream-like passages of the novel. A robot that quotes Robert Burns, and a Samuel Johnson-meets-Frankenstein scenario are representative instances of the novel's comic inventiveness.

Already in the first paragraph of the novel, the author alerts the reader to the layered meanings of the prose (corresponding to the levels of being – the layered realities – that comprise the universe) by alluding to Alfred, Lord Tennyson's "Come Down, O Maid", and W.B. Yeats's "The Lake Isle of Innisfree". Certain of the literary allusions thereafter are merely playful, while others are more pertinent to the structure and meaning of the novel, as when in the opening pages of the first chapter, Helena reads the titles of the books in Paradine's personal library, certain of which – such as Boswell's *Life of Johnson* and T.H. White's *The Once and Future King* – prefigure sequences later in the novel.

Together with the allusion to Plato's allegory of the cavern that occurs in the sequence where Kraag exists as a blind cave-dwelling creature, and in the recurrent references to the visionary works of William Blake made throughout the novel, the most pertinent literary allusion that occurs in *The Hole in the Zero* is that made to John Keats's unfinished masterpiece, *The Fall of Hyperion: A Dream*, written in 1819.

Drawing on Greek mythology, Keats's epic poem concerns the period of transition from the rule of the primeval Titans to that of the rule of the Olympians, during which the Titan Hyperion is displaced as god of the sun by the Olympian Apollo. The structure of the poem is that of a dream within a dream, with the final revelation and ultimate enlightenment of the poet-narrator taking place in a vision in a dream within a dream.

The parallels between Keats's poem and *The Hole in the Zero* are significant to a full understanding of the latter work. Clearly, the essential structure of dream-worlds within dream-worlds is much the same in both works and serves in both the same thematic end, that of a portrayal of the role of the human imagination and its relation to truth. The relationship between the Titan

Hyperion and the Olympian Apollo manifests itself in *The Hole in the Zero* in the rivalry between Hyperion Merganser and Paradine – with Merganser embodying the primal instincts and Paradine personifying the higher qualities of the mind and spirit.

In *The Hole in the Zero*, Merganser is ultimately displaced by Paradine because Paradine is, so to speak, the truer sun god, shining not with the hot sensual brilliance of Merganser, but with the clear light of an inward sun, the radiance of the visionary imagination. This inner star (as Paracelsus named it) or inward sun is that referred to in the quotation from Plotinus that is recalled in his extremity by Paradine and which inspires him to recreate the universe by an act of imagination: "The eye could not behold the sun if its essence were not formed like the sun." (190)

Both *The Fall of Hyperion* and *The Hole in the Zero* employ the rite-of-passage or initiation motif as a vehicle for affirming the centrality of imaginative vision in the spiritual life of humankind. Similarly, both works regard the life of the universe as a process, a progression, each stage of cosmic evolution proceeding from the destructtion of the preceding stage. In *The Hole in the Zero* the evolving consciousness of the universe as expressed through human consciousness is configured in the conflict between the paired opposites, on one side, Kraag and Merganser with their base and selfish dreams, and, on the other side, Helena and Paradine with their self-transcending ideals of harmony, order, beauty and truth.

However, as the novel's concluding sentence – "increase and multiply, my children, and replenish the earth" – with its Biblical resonances, uttered by the thunder *"to itself"* (emphasis mine) suggests, the new cycle that has been initiated is not yet the final one but only a higher one than that immediately preceding. The universe will have to pass through further successive, progressive cycles of dissolution and renewal before ultimate unity beyond being, in the One, is achieved.

The essential situation and the locus of *The Hole in the Zero,* the plight of four figures marooned in the void, may be seen, of course, as a metaphor for the predicament of humanity, similarly cast up on the desolate coast of physical existence where material reality assumes endlessly unpredictable shapes. The alternate courses and fates of the characters in the novel, their predilections and preferences, their decisions and elections, are likewise those which humankind must meet and with which it must contend, again and again, as in cycle after cycle of human history it confronts doom or redemption.

The Hole in the Zero is a many-faceted, serio-comic, slyly subversive yet ultimately numinous view of the great absolutes. With wit and inventiveness the novel dramatises perennial philosophical issues, presenting them to the reader in the guise of a symbol-laden, cosmic-chaotic journey among lurid interior landscapes and hallucinatory scenes of carnage and desolation, prospects exciting malaise and terror yet inspiring also a kind of fearful reverence. It is a work distinguished by a quirky originality of conception and by skill and ingenuity in execution, mixing impish humour and poetic suggestion, oneiric mystery, poignant beauty and pointed satire with visionary mysticism. Amusing and fascinating, *The Hole in the Zero* has the power to make the reader consider afresh the ultimate questions.

The Hole in the Zero
by M.K. Joseph
Victor Gollancz, London, 1967.

AN INWARD ICE-AGE:
ICE

Nearly forty years after its publication in 1967, Anna Kavan's novel, *Ice,* was reprinted in 2006. Since, however, fifteen years later, the value of this admirable novel has yet to be properly recognized, I have chosen to include it here among my selection of neglected books.

Critics of Anna Kavan's *Ice* acknowledge unanimously the centrality to the meaning of the novel of the text's recurrent imagery of ice and cold. There is, however, rather less agreement as to the metaphoric implications of that imagery and its significance for the theme of the novel. Brian W. Aldiss, Christopher Priest, Jeremy Reed and Victoria Nelson concur in seeing the ice and cold imagery as a metaphor for the author's addiction to heroin. This interpretation is endorsed by Abigail Nussbaum, who in addition to the heroin metaphor also sees in the imagery a suggestion of Anna Kavan's "struggle with mental illness." Janet Byrne also emphasizes parallels between Kavan's personal life and figures in *Ice*, characterizing the narrator of the novel as "a direct expression of Kavan's thoughts and feelings," and as representing "Kavan's mouthpiece." At the same time, the central female figure of *Ice* is also seen by Byrne to be "a projection of Kavan."

Beyond such strictly biographical readings of the novel, there are historically grounded explications that consider Kavan's *Ice* as giving expression to cultural or political criticism. Aldiss, for example, states his belief that apart from its immediate biographical level of meaning, *Ice* constitutes a parable of "totalitarianism." L. Trimmel Duchamp regards the novel as depicting "an inexorable vision of the Cold War world ... a surrealist bead on the Cold War reality of the 1960s." And in a similar vein, Kate Zambreno construes *Ice* as an expression of the author's consternation at the accelerating, intensifying horrors of the twentieth century, the encroaching ice symbolizing in Kavan's imagination "the transformation of a world that had ceased to be rooted in reason." The range of suggestion encompassed by the imagery of is sufficiently extensive to accommodate all of the above readings. I believe, however, that a deeper significance underlies the various interpretations offered by the above-mentioned critics. There is another level of reading at which the central characters of *Ice* may be seen to suggest the conflicting components of the human psyche. Accordingly, the events of the novel – the patterns of attraction and repulsion, flight and pursuit that are enacted among the central characters – may be understood to represent a process of psychic development conducing to the end of self-integration. Viewed in this manner, the imagery of cold and ice that so permeates the novel ultimately takes on associations with inward psychic states.

The theme of *Ice* and the significance of its supporting imagery are, then, best approached through an understanding of the three central figures of the novel and their relations to each other.

The central and most complex figure in *Ice* is the nameless narrator. But in order to comprehend the tensions that inform his character, it is first necessary to understand the nature of the other figures in the novel with whom he interacts: his powerful dark-hearted rival, and the luminous elusive girl.

The figure of the rival is comprised of two closely-related characters in the novel, -- the painter-husband and the warden – of which the latter may be seen as a further, fuller development of the former. The painter possesses a dual aspect. Outwardly, he appears amiable, cordial, full of tender concern for his wife – "the girl" as she is referred to throughout the novel. Inwardly, however, he is suspicious, vindictive, cunning. He employs his sincere, civilized manner as a way of attempting to entrap others, encouraging them to reveal their innermost thoughts, as when in conversation with the narrator he attempts to draw him out, to trick him into admissions with regard to the nature of his former relationship to the girl. Even the painter's dilettantish practice of his art is but a ruse for a kind of voyeurism and the exercise of power over his models. The true character of the painter is revealed in his attempt to murder the narrator during the ascent of the old tower that the painter has lured him into climbing.

This hidden but dominant aspect of the painter's nature becomes more pronounced during the narrator's second visit to his house. Upon this occasion the painter makes little effort to disguise his suspicions and his hostility, indulging to the fullest his malicious humour and his overbearing manner, bullying his wife, insulting his guest. And whereas in the interim between the narrator's two visits, the painter has become "heavier, harder, tougher" in appearance, the girl has grown thinner and "more nearly transparent," – as if in the manner of a psychic parasite he has drawn his nourishment from her energies, her substance. The military overcoat that the painter wears on this occasion suggests the full emergence of his brutal, violent character, and serves also to prefigure his subsequent reincarnation in the novel as the warden.

The painter disappears from the novel shortly after the girl's escape from him, but soon reappears in the same chapter of the book in the figure of the warden. More so even than the morose, malevolent, jealously possessive painter, the warden represents the embodiment and the epitome of all that is most selfish in the human character, the incarnation of predation, calculation, deceit, and the unrestrained craving for power.

The reader's first view of the figure of the warden is of a man whose immaculate military apparel and arrogant bearing bespeak a cold, casual, accustomed exercise of command and control over others. Imperiously, he assumes possession of the girl. Like the painter, the warden has a dual aspect, combining a certain refinement of appearance and deportment with an intense, resolute will-to-power. The warden smiles but in his voice there is the hint of a threat. He links arms with the girl, "apparently friendly, but really forcing her forward against her will."

Like the painter, the warden also employs cunning in his relations to others, seeming at times by his manner to express solicitude for others only to betray them when they have revealed themselves to him. To an even greater degree than the painter, the warden is a duplicitous and dangerous man, one whose appreciation of beauty derives from his desire to be in sole and exclusive possession of beautiful things. For the warden the possession of the beautiful – whether the girl or a garden – is a form of self-aggrandizement, an exercise of power.

Through the greater part of the story it is the warden who is in possession of the girl, keeping her close confined in his fortress, while the narrator pursues them from land to land in the hope of luring her away from the warden, rescuing her from him, or even abducting her. There is between the two men a fierce rivalry, each attempting to deceive and out-maneuver the other in order to gain or to retain possession of the girl. Their rivalry at last assumes a deadly character when the warden –like the painter before him – attempts to eliminate his competitor. In the end, the narrator triumphs over his rival, saving the girl from the cruel warden, but in order to accomplish his rescue of her the narrator must undergo an inner transformation, achieve insight into himself and his motives, and learn to understand the motive for the girl's behaviour toward him.

For her part, the girl regards both men as her oppressors, as rival tyrants whose common goal is to dominate and to torment her. Although she resists the role of victim, it is the part that has been forced upon her since childhood. She has been bullied through her childhood and adolescence by her mother "who kept her in a permanent state of frightened subjection," conditioning her to obedience, and forcing her into "a victim's pattern of thought and behaviour." Imbued with a sense of fatality, she yet retains a certain degree of initiative and a disposition to resist.

On the one hand, she submits to the domineering behaviour of the painter and the warden, defenceless against their aggressive wills. Yet on the other hand, she contrives to escape from both men, evincing no small adroitness and ingenuity in doing so. Her fragile but resolute sense of personal dignity and her will to resist manifest themselves also in her behaviour toward the narrator. Wounded by his presumptuous, peremptory manner, the girl expresses her defiance and resistance through her studied aloofness toward him.

In spite of all that has been done to extinguish her spirit, despite the morbid sensitivity and timidity that are the result of her upbringing, the girl's essential nature expresses itself in a capacity for sympathy and in her aesthetic inclinations – she offers aspirin to the narrator for his headache despite the painter's glowering disapproval and the threat of retribution it betokens, she decorates her bare, cold room with pieces of driftwood and delicately coloured sea-shells she has found. And although domination and ill-treatment by others have instilled in her habits of distrust and wariness, she opens when she finds herself in a congenial atmosphere, as when she is brought to the equatorial town with its warmth, its colour and music, and its bright and lively atmosphere. There she unfolds like a flower. Similarly, despite her deeply wounded feelings and her fears, she blossoms in an instant under the sudden sincere tenderness and affection shown her at last by the narrator.

The narrator's final, decisive assumption of the role of protector and lover of the girl, occurring in the last pages of the novel, represents the outcome of a prolonged and intense struggle that has taken place in his mind and spirit, a contest between the inferior, ignoble traits of his character and his higher, worthier qualities. This inward struggle enacted by the narrator is objectified or emblematized in the novel by his relationship to the other central figures in the story – the warden and the girl.

Upon the occasion of their first encounter there is between the narrator and the warden an immediate, if distant, antipathy. The narrator dislikes the warden for his arrogant manner; while for his part the warden senses and resents the narrator's disapproval of him. Upon their next meeting, however, the two men achieve an odd sort of psychic rapport. The narrator is on this occasion altogether more favourably impressed by his rival, reflecting that: "In spite of my original aversion, I suddenly had a curious sense of contact with him, as though some personal link existed between us."

The narrator's sense of an obscure kind of sympathy and intimacy between the warden and himself grows in strength during the course of their subsequent contacts with each other. Despite the warden's employment of subterfuges and stratagems designed to discourage the narrator and thus to retain for himself possession of the girl, the narrator yet feels toward the warden an emotion that he characterizes as "an indescribable affinity, a sort of blood-contact, generating confusion so that I began to wonder if there *were* two of us." Later, this unaccountable, undesired sense of kinship and likeness intensifies to an ever greater degree:

"In an indescribable way our looks tangled together. I seemed to be looking at my own reflection. Suddenly I was entangled in utmost confusion, not sure which of us was which. We were like halves of one being, joined in some mysterious symbiosis. I fought to retain my identity, but all my efforts failed to keep us apart. I continually found I was not myself but him. At one moment I actually seemed to be wearing his clothes."

The persistent, powerful feeling on the part of the narrator that he is linked intimately with the warden, that they are "like twin brothers" reaches its most extreme degree in the moment just preceding the warden's betrayal of him, delivering the narrator to be brutally murdered at the hands of the warden's personal retinue of vicious thugs. In that vertiginous moment when the narrator comprehends the warden's treachery, he also understands that there has never been a bond between himself and the warden, that his sense of identification with his rival was a complete and utter misapprehension.

Yet it is not only the narrator who has perceived a significant similitude of character between the two men. The phenomenon is also noted and acted upon by the girl, who perceives in them an essential likeness: their capacity for cruelty, selfishness and treachery. At one point when the narrator proposes to her that they flee together from the warden, the girl objects that to do so would be pointless since for her there is no difference between the two men. On another later occasion, the girl accuses the narrator of being in league with the warden, and though the narrator denies the accusation, he cannot dismiss it, admitting to himself that "in a strange way there seemed to be some truth in the charge."

The affinity between the warden and narrator that is felt by the narrator and perceived by the girl derives from the darker aspects of the narrator's psyche: his selfish and sadistic tendencies. These impulses distemper and distort his deeper affection for the girl, perverting his purposes and causing him to perplex and affront her with his equivocal actions.

The reader first becomes aware of the narrator's darker appetites when early in the novel the narrator hallucinates seeing the girl naked and terrified, trapped among encroaching cliffs of ice. In this fantasy the narrator feels no pity for her plight, but rather derives "an indescribable pleasure from seeing her suffer." Subsequently, encountering her in person, sensations of a similar character are provoked in him by what he names the "victim's look" of her face, a hint of bruising around the eyes that he finds "madly attractive."

Clearly attracted to the idea of inflicting erotic pain on the girl, of possessing her as a victim, the narrator projects onto her his own temptation, imagining that she solicits her own victimization. Disapproving of his own sadistic impulses and disclaiming any desire to realize them, he blames her for evoking in him such cravings: "she corrupted my dreams, led me into dark places I had no wish to explore." Ultimately, he comes to act out elements of his darkly desired scenario of erotic domination. Having abducted the girl by force to accompany him on a journey to a warmer climate, and tiring of her petulance, he strikes her face. Thereafter, he intimidates her with a menacing silence like that employed against the girl by her former captor, the warden: "I ... adopted the warden's silences as my own. I was well aware how sinister my wordless exits and entrances must have seemed, and derived some satisfaction from this."

Yet there is another contrasting aspect to the narrator's urgent, persistent preoccupation with the girl. Just as the narrator sometimes fantasizes of inflicting pain and injury on the girl, so too he fantasizes of rescuing her from danger, delivering her from confinement and captivity. Early in the novel, for example, before the character of the global catastrophe is known, the narrator experiences a premonitory hallucination in which he envisions the rapid advance of giant ice-cliffs entrapping the girl, threatening to crush her. In this vision – in distinction to that in which he savours her suffering – the narrator runs to rescue her from the ice, calling out to her not to be frightened, promising to save her. Similarly, the narrator's repeated efforts in the course of the novel to find her and liberate her from the control of the warden or to save her from unpleasant or perilous circumstances bespeak a regard on his part for her safety and happiness, a solicitous concern that clearly goes beyond both rivalry with the warden and erotic fascination with the girl.

The narrator's obsession with the girl seems to derive much of its motive power from an instinctual attraction that is mysterious in character, yet may be seen to be related to the constitution of the human psyche. The unaccountable, irrational, compulsive urge that drives the narrator to abandon all his other duties and affairs and repeatedly to search for the girl springs from a profound unitive impulse, a powerful craving to recover wholeness of being. As the narrator attempts to express this self-integrative drive, the imperative need he feels to find and to keep the girl is one "as for a missing part of myself," and "as for a lost, essential portion of my own being."

Again and again, when forced apart from the girl, the narrator feels that he cannot bear separation from her, cannot live without her presence. On one occasion, when in despair at losing her once again, he momentarily considers abandoning the search for her and using his remaining time in cultivating a more peaceful mode of life, he immediately dismisses the notion: "No, that was impossible. I was tied to her."

Following the narrator's final revelatory encounter with the warden, which results in the narrator becoming at last disabused of the notion that there is between the warden and himself a kind of affinity, the narrator begins to be free of confusion concerning his motives and desires. Immediately, he feels once more an intense attraction to the girl, a compulsive urge to see her again, to reach her before the warden can find her.

The narrator's urgent desire to reach the girl – an impulse that impels him through many perils and ordeals – derives both from a feeling of attraction to her and from a wish to save her from the power of the warden, to prevent her being recaptured by the warden and becoming again subject to his cruel and oppressive control. In psychic terms, this new course undertaken by the narrator represents a decisive change of direction. After confronting and coming to terms with his selfish, animal impulses – as embodied in the figure of the warden – the narrator can now turn toward the expression of unselfish concern and affection. The process of refinement that the narrator undergoes is one in which he must overcome, reject and repudiate that aspect of himself represented by the warden, and recognize, value and embrace that aspect represented by the girl.

The process of inner transformation on the part of the narrator is completed when at length he finds the girl, is rebuffed by her, determines at first to abandon her to her fate, but then sets aside his pride and anger and gives expression to his compassion and tender concern for her. In an open-hearted, sincere exchange with the girl – corresponding in an opposite manner to the narrator's earlier confrontation with the warden – the narrator recognizes the truth concerning his former domineering behaviour toward the girl, and the truth also concerning his deepest feelings for her. With shame and regret he acknowledges the role of bully and oppressor that he has played in relation to her, apologizing to her for his possessive, assertive, selfish actions.

At last the narrator is able to give full expression to his repressed feelings of tenderness for the girl, realizing that his profound affection for her was continually distorted and deflected by his base, selfish appetites – impulses which now have been vanquished in him. The narrator's long struggle with himself is resolved, his inward transformation is complete.

In the affectionate union of the girl and the narrator the power of the unitive urge of the self is affirmed. The narrator's impulse toward union with the luminous girl, the soul-image, the embodiment of the higher and nobler human instincts, has proven stronger ultimately than the dark attractions of the primitive, uncontrolled, animal aspects of the psyche, as embodied in the warden. Like the bewitched prince in the fairy tale of Beauty and the Beast, the narrator is liberated and transformed by love, and through love he is at last united with the "lost, essential portion of his own being" for which he has been searching.

The theme of self-division and self-integration, of the inner struggle between impulses of selfishness and destructiveness and motives of compassion and love, as represented in the novel through the relationship among the three central characters, provides the context in which the novel's recurrent motif of cold and ice may be understood. The new and final ice-age whose implacable progress during the course of the novel constitutes the determining circumstance of the story, has as its immediate cause the testing of powerful nuclear weapons. These weapons themselves are, of course, an expression of human suspicion, competition and destructiveness. In the novel, the outer echoes the inner. In this manner, the ice-age and all-obliterating cold may be seen as an externalization of human emotional coldness, an outward manifestation of collective human destructiveness. The glacial chill that permeates Kavan's *Ice* corresponds to and proceeds from the cold waste places within; the ice-age is born in the frozen human heart.

Evidence for such a perspective on the imagery of icy disaster in the novel is to be found in the link that is suggested in the text between the figure of the warden and the nature of the catastrophe. Both the warden and the catastrophe share the attributes of destructive power and complete indifference to the lives and feelings of others. More specifically, throughout the novel, the cruel, ruthless warden is described in terms of cold and ice. Upon his first appearance in the novel, the warden's eyes are likened by the narrator to "startling pieces of bright blue ice." Later, the narrator notes "the cold white of his long, thin restless hands," and his "ice eyes." The warden is said to have an "icy voice ... a cold voice" that states things "coldly." And, again, his is a "look of ice" with eyes compared to "arrows of blue ice piercing a blizzard."

The implied link between the warden who is the embodiment of all that is base in humankind and the cataclysm of cold and ice serves to suggest that the new ice-age is a modern parallel to the Biblical deluge in that it is a consequence of the misdeeds of the human race. Human emotional coldness, selfishness and destructiveness, denial of empathy and withholding of compassion, have provoked an appropriate response from nature or from whatever are the laws or ruling forces of the universe. Humankind is being paid back in kind; its collective transgressions have reacted upon it in the form of poetic justice. The punishment, we may say, fits the crime: coldness of heart has brought about universal cold. As the narrator sadly reflects:

"The ultimate achievement of mankind would be, not just self-destruction, but the destruction of all life; the transformation of the living world into a dead planet. ... I was oppressed ... by the enormity of what had been done, the weight of collective guilt. A frightful crime had been committed, against nature, against the universe, against life. By rejecting life, man had destroyed the immemorial order, destroyed the world."

As if to confirm the justification of the annihilation of the human race, during the course of cataclysm the human tendencies toward ruthless self-interest and destructiveness are given ever greater rein. Warfare breaks out among the various nations of the earth, uprisings take place. Everywhere oppressive authoritarian regimes assume power. Desperate hordes of starving refugees engage in rampages of looting and pillaging. The aged and helpless are abandoned. Barbarism and atavism increasingly prevail. The warden is not a unique phenomenon. He may be the epitome of selfishness, cold lust and the will to power, but there is, the novel suggests, a warden in every human heart.

That such tendencies can be resisted, overcome and transformed into compassion and love, that we can succeed in realizing our truest, deepest human potentials, as suggested by the growing self-awareness and ultimate transformation of the narrator, is the heartening message of Anna Kavan's cautionary tale; that such a transformation is unlikely and that it is probably already too late for humanity anyway would seem to be the novel's more disconsolate conclusion.

Ice by Anna Kavan
Peter Owen, London, 1967.
Reprinted in paperback
by Picador, London, 1973.

KATABASIS:
Post Bellum Blues

From his native Ireland to war-ravaged, occupied Germany, from Germany across the sea to the United States, from stockade to prison, and from prison to prison, then back at last to Ireland, *Post Bellum Blues* by Finn MacMahon is the first-person account of a young soldier, his missteps, his misfortunes, his dark downward journey. Having set forth from his home in a spirit of adventure three years previously, he returns there destitute and in disrepute, a deportee from the Land of the Free, a fiasco and an outcast, a penniless ex-jailbird with a dishonourable discharge from the U.S. Army, yet hidden within his breast he bears rare and precious treasures: strength, dignity and integrity.

The author begins his memoir during a rainy winter in the county Kerry, Ireland, when he is a restless and naive eighteen year old who dreams of seeking his fortune on the Gold Coast of Africa, imagining adventures there among jungles, mountain lakes and brightly-colored birds. Warned off such an undertaking by his father and an old man who has seen the Gold Coast in all its unwholesomeness and sordidness, young Finn is persuaded (by his father, an old cavalryman) to enlist, instead, in the U.S. Army. Owing to his father's former service in the U.S. Army, Finn is permitted to take an oath of allegiance at the U.S. Consulate in Cobh. He then travels to London where he takes an oath of enlistment, is issued a uniform, and whence he then travels to an army replacement depot in Germany. The year is 1946, only eight months after the German defeat, and the country is in ruins and desperately poor, operating on what one ex-GI (Edward Darringhaus in Studs Terkel's *The Good War)* remembered as a "cigarette butt economy," that is "when we flipped our cigarette butts in the gutter, the kids jumped on it. Three butts would make one cigarette and that was enough to buy something to eat." After receiving only four hours of basic training, Finn is assigned to his duty station, a Quartermaster unit near Friedburg.

Finn is unaware that he brings with him into his career as a soldier an invisible interior adversary, an inner antagonist. As we, as readers, gradually become aware, he has been traumatized by his experiences as an adolescent during the blitz in London where he lived with his mother and siblings: wounded in mind by the fury of aerial bombardment, by witnessing the devastation of whole quarters, by the mutilated dead lying in the streets, by the V-1 and V-2 rockets raining down randomly and terrifyingly on the city, and most deeply damaged by the death of his beloved older brother.

To suppress and evade the intense emotional aftershocks of his traumatic adolescent years, young Finn drinks frequently and to excess. At age eighteen, he is already an incipient alcoholic. Early indications of his psychological state are to be found in the opening pages of his memoir. In the course of an argument with his father, for example, the father, speaking truer than he knows, caustically remarks: "Those doodle-bugs in London must have scattered what brains you had all over John Bull's island." We learn, too, that Finn – though unconscious of their profound impact on him – is haunted by harrowing memories of the war years in London. "My mind," he writes, "was full of grey dust, visions of ruins, screaming bombs, shattered nights, broken walls and finally of a white cross in an English field where my brother John was sleeping his endless sleep."

In an offhand fashion, Finn recounts the drinking bouts he undertakes both during the days immediately before and in the hours after appearing at the American consul in Cobh to take his oath. Indeed, during that visit to the consul, his head is so befuddled with drink that he is uncertain of the nature of the oath he has sworn: "I vaguely remember taking some kind of oath in front of the flag." He leaves the consul, heading for the pub, in the mistaken belief that he has now become an American citizen, later identifying himself as such on official forms, an error that will later work to his considerable detriment.

To his disappointment, MacMahon – who relished the prospect of physical challenges – discovers that military discipline at Friedburg barracks is nearly non-existent and that there seems to be little in the way of actual duties to perform. The war is over and officers and enlisted men alike are merely marking time and waiting to be shipped home. Bored, he soon falls in with a rowdy, hard-drinking lot, spending every evening intoxicated on cheap brandy and in bed with one or another of a wide range of willing women, from WACs to German war widows.

Drunken brawls and mad pranks eventually lead to a reprimand and mild punishment from his commanding officer. But MacMahon's prodigious consumption of liquor continues apace, escalating until he and his drinking companions begin to drink schnapps or brandy before breakfast, noting with some dismay that half a bottle is required to stop their hands from shaking. In a seizure of liquor-fueled madness, Finn and his best friend nearly murder each other in a fight one drunken night. On another occasion, Finn exchanges pistol shots with a German in a darkened street. One of their drinking buddies goes berserk and has to be restrained with straps and shipped home. MacMahon begins to pass out from drinking and to suffer alcoholic lacunae. While drunk, though, vivid memories of the blitz and his brother's death surface, and he becomes attracted to the idea of committing sucide. Restricted to quarters by his commanding officer, following an incident, MacMahon disregards orders, flees and is shot at and beaten by the military police. He is court-martialled and sentenced to six months in the stockade.

Existence in the stockade at Schweinfurt is reduced to hours of callisthenics followed by hour upon hour of close order drill, long hours of scrubbing floors, tables, walls and doors, and recurrent inspections and formations, some in the middle of the night. The food is poor, the beds are but wooden planks, the prison uniforms are thin and insufficiently warm during the deep frozen winter months. From pre-dawn to dark, every moment of the day, every aspect of life is regulated. For infractions of the rules, MacMahon is subjected to punishment drill, marching and double-timing while humping on his back a pack filled with 60 pounds of sand. He also endures a week in solitary confinement: living in darkness and silence in a frigid, underground cell, subsisting on bread and water.

At Schweinfurt, Finn witnesses violence and brutality, both inflicted upon and practiced among his fellow-prisoners. His six month term in the stockade is a stark lesson in elementary human psychology: some men are equable and tolerant, seeking only mutual co-existence, other men are vicious and pitiless, craving power and relishing the subjugation of others. And, as effectively as possible, incurring as few inward fractures as possible, a man must navigate this dangerous world.

Sadly, though, from this misadventure, Finn learns little more than that, achieving no insight into his self-destructive behaviour. Upon release from the stockade and reassignment to his unit – as if he can see no other purpose in life – he quickly resumes his headlong course of hard drinking and fruitless fornication. Only a short time after his release, in a state of extreme inebriation, he assaults a sergeant, is court-martialled and sentenced to three years imprisonment and a dishonourable discharge.

Würtzburg military prison, where MacMahon is then confined is the stockade in starker form: the same oppressive iron-handed discipline, the same monotony and brutality, the same uniformity and coarseness of life, and the same loneliness and invisible miasma of sorrow. Only the humour and stoicism of his fellow prisoners serve to hearten him. After several months incarceration at Würtzburg, Finn is transferred to a military correctional facility in the state of Connecticut, then transferred again to another facility where he completes his sentence. On the day of his scheduled release, he is held until he can be arrested by the U.S. Immigration Service. The charge (incredibly, considering that Macmahon set foot in the United States under armed guard) is entering the country illegally.

The staggering absurdity of the situation would be comical were it not so calamitous. For his involuntary violation of the Immigration Act, MacMahon is immediately re-incarcerated in a federal prison. There he languishes for months while his case (which he does not appeal) proceeds with excruciating slowness through the justice system. By this time, he is worn thin in mind and spirit. He becomes listless. He rages. He is afflicted with anxiety attacks. At last, released and then taken to the detention center on Ellis Island, he is deported to his native Ireland, disembarking at Cobh, where three bleak years previously he swore the oath of allegiance that he thought granted him American citizenship. He is now but a short distance from his home in Cork City. His sad, circular journey is complete. Although he returns to his homeland "in disgrace with fortune and men's eyes," inwardly he remains intact and as he prepares to set his feet on earth of home, feels happiness and hope.

From his descent into the underworld of unconstrained appetite, dark impulse, punishment and incarceration, Finn MacMahon brings back with him a self-formulated personal code to live by, a perspective on life and the world, and a balm for his war-wounded spirit. His *Post Bellum Blues* is, indeed, a blues in the sense that Ralph Ellison has defined the genre: "The blues is an impulse to keep the painful details and episodes of a brutal experience alive in ones aching consciousness ... and to transcend it ... the blues is an autobiographical chronicle of personal catastrophe expressed lyrically." (*Living with Music: Jazz Writings* by Ralph Ellison.)

Finn's code consists of a set of private ideals, chief among which is that of not accepting the oppressive exercise of power either by authority or by other persons. He refuses to surrender to others his sense of agency, he will not be intimidated, he will not submit or acquiesce. He insists upon his independence. This is the core of his integrity. If another attempts to violate his rights as an individual, he will confront the would-be persecutor, he will resist, whatever the cost. The clearest instance of such behaviour is MacMahon's refusal to accept a gig and extra drill from Polson, the "little tin god" trusty at Würtzburg prison. In a similar manner, MacMahon later disdains to bend or buckle under to the exhausting punishment inflicted upon him by another brutal prison trusty: "Go on, you bastard, scream your head off all night, I thought. You'll never break me in a thousand years." The ultimate and most decisive instance of this same attitude of defiant self-determination occurs when – after years of harsh imprisonment – he is offered the opportunity by an army reviewing board to avoid a dishonourable discharge and to remain in the army. To the surprise of the board, he declines. "The last thing in the world I felt at that moment was repentance," he writes, "I expected no favours and wanted none."

Finn does, however, accept as his due, without complaint or self-pity, his judicial punishment, though he declines to be complicit in the punishment of others, twice while imprisoned refusing advantageous positions as a trusty. Crucially, belatedly, he also recognizes that his misdeeds have serious consequences for other people: his sisters and his mother who fret over his fate. From his initial insouciant approach to life – "all I could think of was women and drink" – he comes to consider the impact of his actions on those who love him. When at Würtzburg prison he receives a visit from his mother and sister, he remarks that seeing their dear faces, "I suddenly felt unclean and I realized for the first time with a shock that I was a *real* criminal, not because I'd frightened some sergeant with a knife, but because I'd brought sorrow and pain to two people whom I loved." Again, on a later occasion when he is invited by a fellow-inmate to join in criminal activity, he declines, reflecting on his family: "I couldn't risk causing them any more pain."

Indeed, earlier, at what is perhaps the most critical, most fateful moment of his life, when driven by drunken fury and prey to a suicidal urge, Finn stands raving and cursing, knife in hand, before two M.P.s with their pistols drawn, it is love that saves him. He was, he writes, at that pivotal moment "consumed with a desire to end everything once and for all." But then, "for no earthly reason, I see my mother's face, clearly, her dark, patient eyes, sad face." Tears blind him and he drops the knife from his hand and is arrested rather than shot. On a later occasion, in a state of acute despondency and near madness, a vision of his dead brother affords peace to his tormented mind. As in so many captivity narratives and stories of personal salvation, it is love that is the efficient cause and instrument bringing new clarity to Mac-Mahon's muddled mind, redeeming him from inward darkness. More powerful than the pleasure principle, more potent than the rage for oblivion, is the action of love upon the spirit.

As suggested in the preceding paragraph, Finn's protean inner antagonist also assumes the shape of cosmic despair. There are two occasions on which he feels himself nearly annihilated by a sense of the insignificance of his own life in a universe devoid of meaning. Once, while in solitary confinement, he is overwhelmed by an image of himself as "an ant, lost in a speck of a world, whirling endlessly among the other specks, the sun, the moon and the planets." Later, in the state of despondency referred to in the paragraph above, he is seized by a sudden terror, the like of which he has never before experienced: "I saw myself as I truly was, a speck in the infinite vastness of the universe." In contrast to such assaults of ontological anxiety, there is an episode when he feels an intimation of an ultimate wholeness of self to be attained in time yet to come. Incongruously, the feeling arises immediately after he has been sentenced to a three year term in prison. "I'd braced myself for a shock but I was caught unawares," he writes, "then, to my complete surprise, something deep inside me took charge of my body and emotions and marched me out of the room. The *real* me was in complete control at that moment. I knew that eventually the real me would be master, and I longed for the day to arrive." The dawn of that day takes place in the choppy wake of his second experience of cosmic terror. For the first time, he records, "I searched my soul and reviewed my past with disgust. What a fool I'd been! My gods had been drink, sex and anarchy." From this moment forward, he puts forth effort to reform his life, to exercise self-control and to practice compassion, though his resolve is at times sorely tested by the vexatious conditions in which he is forced to live.

Aside from its psychological interest as a chronicle of initiation and inner transformation, *Post Bellum Blues* is eminently worthy of attention for its vivid record of a time and a place – postwar Germany with its shattered towns, maimed ex-Wehrmacht soldiers and desperate women – and for its finely rendered portraits of a range of characters who drift in and out of the author's memoir: drunken, damaged veterans, eccentrics, deserters, sadistic trusties, brutal guards, illegal aliens, unbroken losers and lost souls. To all of this, Finn Macmahon is a unique witness.

There are things of which – had Finn MacMahon not been there to see them and later to record them – we should never have known. Curious, poignant particulars of life on this dark earth. Graffiti scratched by men's fingernails into the brick wall of a cell once occupied by prisoners condemned to death by the Nazis: names and dates, prayers and farewells. The sad dignity of a doomed young American soldier soon to be hanged for murder. The smirking hubris of a psychotic, chess-obsessed, cold-blooded killer. Scruffy German children begging G.I.s for cigarettes and chocolate amid the rubble of cities. Old soldiers such as Maguire and "Pop" Grant, whose quirky spirit and vivid individuality serve as a rebuke to banality. An ardent, raving sermon delivered to inmates by a half-mad backwoods preacher. A decorated company commander court-martialed for deliberately shooting one of his own men. Luckless yet irrepressibly optimistic prisoners such as toothless Greg a wounded deserter whose refrain of "Boing! Boing! Boing!" seems to suggest that he views his life as a rubber ball bounced up and down by the invisible hand of Fate; and Jethro, an African-American prisoner who – despite adversity and oppressive racial prejudice – remains buoyant and affable: "life had not embittered him ... I envied his gift of thanking God for each day and each small mercy. To him, everything in Nature was a source of pleasure and wonder." Echoes down the long corridor of time, haunting glimpses, baffling fragments, ciphers and hieroglyphs of human life, salient still.

Of Finn Macmahon, I have been able to discover nothing further. I believe the author's name to be a nom-de-plume. On the back panel of the first edition of the book, the following is the only information provided: "Born in Kerry, in January 1946 at the age of 18 he signed on in the U.S. army at the U.S. Consulate in Cobh, and was dishonourably discharged in March 1949." His fluidly written, candid, compelling, memorable memoir published in 1965 – sixteen years after the events the author records – reflects a mind tempered by early suffering and ripened by years of mature reflection. *Post Bellum Blues* is a work of definite and distinct value.

Post Bellum Blues
by Finn MacMahon
The Bodley Head, London, 1965.
Reprinted in paperback format
by Foursquare Books, London, 1967.

www.ingramcontent.com/pod-product-compliance
Lightning Source LLC
LaVergne TN
LVHW050845200726
843507LV00001B/429